I0062676

Money Skills for Young Adults

A Beginner's Guide to Smart Financial Habits, with Simple Tools to Manage Your Budget, Save for Goals, Invest, and Build Your Independent & Secure Future

Pantheon Space Academy

Copyright © 2025

Pantheon Space Academy

MONEY SKILLS FOR YOUNG ADULTS

A Beginner's Guide to Smart Financial Habits, with Simple Tools

to Manage Your Budget, Save for Goals, Invest, and Build

Your Independent & Secure Future

All rights reserved.

No part of this publication may be reproduced, distributed, or transmitted in any form or by any means, including photocopying, recording, or other electronic or mechanical methods, without the prior written permission of the author, except in the case of brief quotations embodied in critical reviews and certain other non-commercial uses permitted by copyright law.

Pantheon Space Academy

Printed Worldwide since 2021

Under no circumstances will any blame or legal responsibility be held against the publisher, or author, for any damages, reparation, or monetary loss due to the information contained within this book. Either directly or indirectly. You are responsible for your own choices, actions, and Results.

Legal Notice:

This book is copyright protected. This book is only for personal use. You cannot amend, distribute, sell, use, quote, or paraphrase any part, or the content within this book, without the consent of the author or publisher.

Disclaimer Notice:

Please note the information contained within this document is for educational and entertainment purposes only. All effort has been executed to present accurate, up-to-date, and reliable, complete information. No warranties of any kind are declared or implied. Readers acknowledge that the author is not engaging in the rendering of legal, financial, medical, or professional advice. The content within this book has been derived from various sources. Please consult a licensed professional before attempting any techniques outlined in this book.

By reading this document, the reader agrees that under no circumstances is the author responsible for any losses, direct or indirect, which are incurred as a result of the use of the information contained within this document, including, but not limited to, — errors, omissions, or inaccuracies.

Money Skills for
Young Adults

Table of Contents

INTRODUCTION

Have you ever logged into your bank account and felt that wave of anxiety, wondering where your hard-earned money went? If you have, you're not alone. Many of us have been there, staring at our finances and thinking, *How did this happen? Where is my money even going?* It's frustrating, confusing, and, honestly, exhausting at times. We've all felt the stress of not knowing if the next bill will throw things off balance or how to juggle everyday expenses with those bigger dreams we have for ourselves.

Here's the thing: managing your money isn't just about crunching numbers or cutting out your favorite coffee. It's about understanding your habits, emotions, and the choices you make with your money. That's what this book is here for: to help you figure it out in a way that actually makes sense for your life. Whether you're just starting your first job, trying to stretch a family budget, or managing student loans, you'll find something in these pages that speaks to you.

Now, imagine waking up without that nagging financial stress and knowing exactly where your money is going, covering your expenses, and still making room for the things that light you up. Picture paying off debt not with drastic sacrifices, but with manageable steps that still let you enjoy life. Or building savings that feel like a safety net you can count on, giving you more freedom and less worry. That's what we're working toward here: real solutions for real life.

Let me introduce you to Sarah. She's someone a lot of us can relate to. Payday used to bring her more dread than relief because she knew it meant divvying up her paycheck to cover bills that left her with barely anything to enjoy life. She tried quick fixes, cutting back on small things, hoping for a raise, but the stress lingered. Then she decided to take a different approach. Instead of scrambling every month, she got clear on where her money was going and built a plan that fit her lifestyle. Fast forward, Sarah now owns her own home, travels, and feels confident about her financial future. Her beginning isn't a fairy tale. But it's something you can make happen, too.

This book is designed to meet you exactly where you are and help you build a plan that feels doable, not overwhelming. We'll start with the basics, because let's be honest, some financial terms can sound way more complicated than they are. But the good news is that once you get the hang of them, you'll wonder why nobody explained it like this before. As you gain clarity, you'll build confidence, making those financial decisions a whole lot easier.

We'll explore budgeting methods tailored to diverse lifestyles, recognizing that a universal solution doesn't exist. You'll gain immediate access to practical strategies, particularly useful if your income fluctuates monthly or you're managing finances with a partner or family. The goal here is simple: to help you take action and start seeing real results.

Money management goes beyond numbers; it's deeply tied to your emotions and beliefs. We'll explore how unconscious thoughts, like "I'm bad with money" or guilt over enjoyable purchases, can hinder your financial progress. Together, we'll transform these limiting beliefs into empowering ones.

And as you move forward, I'll help you think about the big picture. Saving for what matters to you, planning for the unexpected, and setting yourself up for long-term success. Whether you're saving for a trip, a new home, or just some peace of mind, you'll find ways to make those goals feel less like distant dreams and more like plans you're actively working toward.

Each chapter offers practical tools and clear steps for immediate application. Upon completion, you'll not only have a budget but a personalized system designed to reduce stress and increase enjoyment. You'll gain the confidence to manage financial challenges and appreciate your progress. For added convenience, the book includes budgeting templates, providing a ready-to-use framework to implement your newfound knowledge instantly.

Take a deep breath and let's do this together. You are capable, and I'll be here to support you in creating a financial life that truly empowers you.

Plus, don't miss the free bonus tools linked at the end of the book!

These include downloadable templates, guides, trackers, and more.

Designed to help you turn knowledge into action.

CHAPTER 1

Understanding Budgeting Basics

D o you ever wonder where your paycheck goes each month, or feel trapped in a spending cycle with little to show for it? Many people do. The solution lies in a solid budget, which provides a clear roadmap for managing your income effectively, saving for your priorities, and reducing unnecessary expenses.

This chapter simplifies the fundamentals of budgeting, making them approachable and practical. You'll discover how to categorize income, track expenses, and establish effective savings strategies. Through real-life examples tailored to various situations, such as early career, fluctuating family income, or managing student loans, you'll gain a solid understanding. By the end, you'll be equipped to create a budget that fosters financial stability, no matter your starting point.

Definitions of Budgeting Terms

To truly master your finances, you must first understand the foundational language of budgeting. A strong comprehension of essential budgeting terminology empowers you to make informed financial choices, maintain organization, and confidently achieve your objectives.

Let's explore the four fundamental components of any effective financial strategy: budget, income, expenses, and savings.

Budget: Your Money Map

A budget is simply a plan for how you're going to use your money. It outlines your expected income (what you earn) and expenses (what you spend) over a specific period, usually a month. If you've ever wondered where your paycheck disappears to, a budget helps you answer that question before the money even leaves your account.

A budget serves as your financial roadmap to freedom. Without it, you risk losing your way through impulse spending, late bill payments, and difficulty saving. However, a well-defined plan allows you to monitor your expenditures precisely and make necessary adjustments to stay on course.

Income: Knowing What You're Working With

Your income is the money you earn, whether from your job, side hustles, government benefits, or passive income sources such as rental properties or dividend investments. The more you understand your total income, the better you can allocate it toward necessities, savings, and goals.

For example, if you have a steady paycheck, budgeting might be easier since you can predict your monthly income. But if you work freelance or part-time, your income may fluctuate, requiring a more flexible approach. Regardless of how your income flows in, tracking every dollar you earn ensures you're making informed financial choices.

Expenses: Where Your Money Goes

Expenses are the costs you incur in daily life, and they fall into two main categories:

- **Fixed Expenses:** These stay the same each month, like rent, insurance, car payments, and subscriptions. Since they're predictable, you can plan for them easily.

- **Variable Expenses:** These change from month to month, like groceries, entertainment, and utilities. While some variation is normal, keeping an eye on these helps you spot areas where you can cut back.

By tracking your expenses, you'll start noticing patterns. Perhaps you're spending more on takeout than you realize, or maybe you can switch to a more affordable phone plan. Understanding these details puts you in control, allowing you to adjust your spending and free up money for things that truly matter.

Savings: Paying Yourself First

Prioritizing your future is key to saving money, not just setting aside what's left over at the end of each month. Whether your goal is an emergency fund, a significant purchase, or retirement investments, a well-structured savings plan is as vital as diligently tracking your expenses.

A smart approach is to consider savings as a fixed expense, an integral and automatic part of your budget, rather than an afterthought. This shift in mindset ensures a consistent allocation of funds toward your future, regardless of other financial happenings.

How It All Comes Together

Let's look at how these concepts work in real life:

- A family creating a budget might start by adding up their total household income, listing out their fixed expenses like mortgage payments and insurance, and categorizing variable expenses like groceries and entertainment. By reviewing their budget, they can decide where to cut back and how much to save each month.

- A student managing their money for the first time might track income from scholarships, part-time jobs, and family support while listing essential expenses like tuition and books. Understanding their spending habits helps them avoid unnecessary debt and start building financial stability early.

- A young professional earning their first full-time paycheck can set up a budget that prioritizes debt repayment, savings, and career development while balancing necessary expenses. By keeping a close eye on income and spending, they can make informed choices that set them up for long-term success.

By learning these key budgeting terms and applying them to your own life, you'll gain control over your finances rather than letting your finances control you.

The Importance of Budgeting

Budgeting isn't merely about tracking numbers; it's the tool that transforms financial chaos into clarity. It empowers you to control your finances, alleviate stress, and ensure your money serves you effectively.

Think of budgeting as your financial game plan. Without one, it's easy to overspend, fall into debt, or struggle to save. But when you actively decide where your money goes, you create opportunities to build stability, meet financial goals, and gain true financial freedom.

Budgeting Brings Awareness

The first step to improving your finances is knowing where your money is going. A budget gives you a clear breakdown of your income and expenses, making it easier to spot problem areas.

You might realize that you're spending more than expected on takeout or online shopping, or that saving is difficult, not because you don't earn enough, but because small, unnecessary expenses are adding up. On the other hand, if you're barely covering bills, a budget can highlight where to cut back or where you may need to explore ways to increase your income.

When you track your money, you take control instead of letting your money control you. That clarity alone can reduce financial stress, making it easier to make wise decisions about spending and saving.

Budgeting Helps You Manage Debt

If you have debt, a budget can help you tackle it head-on. Instead of making random payments and hoping for the best, you can create a structured plan to pay it off faster and with less stress.

By outlining your income and expenses, you can identify extra money to put toward your debts, whether that means cutting back on non-essential spending or reallocating funds more effectively. A budget also allows you to prioritize high-interest debts first, reducing the amount you pay over time. Just as importantly, it helps prevent accidental overspending, ensuring you don't keep falling into the same debt cycle and making it easier to stay on track toward financial freedom.

For example, imagine you're making minimum payments on a student loan while spending a lot on dining out. By redirecting just a small portion of that restaurant budget toward your loan, you could pay it off months (or even years) earlier, saving hundreds or thousands of dollars in interest.

Budgeting Turns Goals into Reality

Want to save for a house? Travel more? Build an emergency fund? Budgeting is what turns those dreams into achievable goals.

When you create a budget, you're not just deciding what to spend—you're intentionally setting aside money for things that matter. A well-planned budget allows you to:

- Save for short-term goals, like a vacation or a new laptop, without feeling guilty about spending.

- Work toward long-term goals, like buying a home or retiring comfortably, without feeling like you're missing out today.

- See real progress, as your savings grow and your goals become more attainable.

A budget makes these goals feel tangible instead of distant wishes. You don't need to be rich to save—you just need a clear plan for your money.

Budgeting Creates Financial Freedom

Many people think budgeting is restrictive, but in reality, it's the key to freedom. When you plan ahead, you:

- Stop living paycheck to paycheck.

- Feel confident about handling emergencies without going into debt.

- Have the ability to say yes to opportunities, instead of worrying about whether you can afford them.

Imagine what it would feel like to not stress over money—to wake up knowing you have enough saved, your bills are covered, and you're moving closer to financial security every day. That's the power of budgeting.

Common Misconceptions about Budgeting

If you've ever thought, *Budgeting isn't for me*, or *Budgets are too restrictive*, you're not the only one. There are plenty of myths about budgeting that make it seem like a rigid, joyless practice—something only the wealthy or ultra-disciplined can maintain. But the truth is, budgeting isn't about taking away your financial freedom; it's about giving you more control over it.

By breaking down some of the most common misconceptions, you'll see that budgeting isn't a punishment—it's an opportunity to make your money work for you, no matter where you are in life.

Misconception #1: Budgeting is Restrictive

A lot of people hear the word "budget" and immediately think of cutting out every little thing they enjoy—no more coffee runs, no weekend outings, no fun at all. But that's not what budgeting is about.

Instead of thinking of a budget as a set of strict rules, imagine it as a flexible spending plan. It's a way to prioritize what matters to you while keeping your finances in check.

Want to grab dinner with friends on the weekend? A budget allows you to plan for it without guilt. Dreaming of a vacation? Setting aside money in advance ensures you can enjoy your trip without sacrificing your everyday needs. Even spontaneous purchases can be part of a budget when you allocate funds for them, giving you the freedom to spend without financial stress.

The key is balance, not elimination. When you create a budget that works with your lifestyle, you're not restricting yourself. You're giving yourself permission to spend, just in a way that aligns with your financial goals.

Misconception #2: Budgeting is Only for the Wealthy

There's a common belief that budgets are only useful if you have a high income or a lot of assets to manage. But in reality, the less money you have, the more important budgeting becomes.

- If you're just starting in your career, a budget helps you stretch every dollar so you're not constantly worrying about making it to the next paycheck.

- If you're a student, budgeting helps you prioritize expenses so you don't overspend on things like dining out while struggling to cover tuition or books.

- If your family's income fluctuates, a budget gives you stability, helping you plan for months when your household income is lower.

Budgeting isn't about how much you make—it's about how you manage what you have. Whether you're earning six figures or working with a tighter budget, having a plan ensures your money is working for you, not against you.

Misconception #3: Budgeting is Too Complicated

Some people think budgeting requires spreadsheet mastery or hours of calculations, but it doesn't have to be that way. The simplest budgets are often the most effective.

- **Step 1:** Know how much money you have coming in.

- **Step 2:** Write down your main expenses (rent, groceries, bills, etc.).

- **Step 3:** Decide how much you want to save and how much you'll spend on extras.

That's it: no advanced math, no complicated formulas. And if tracking every dollar feels overwhelming, some apps can do it for you, some even link to your bank account and categorize your spending automatically.

The point of budgeting isn't perfection—it's awareness. You don't need an accountant-level strategy to make a budget work for you. Start small and adjust as needed.

Misconception #4: Once You Set a Budget, It's Set in Stone

A budget isn't something you create once and follow forever. Life changes—and so should your budget.

Think about it:

- If you get a raise, wouldn't you adjust your savings or spending?

- If an unexpected expense pops up, wouldn't you want the flexibility to cover it?

- If your goals shift, wouldn't you want to change where your money is going?

A good budget is a flexible budget. It's something you review and tweak regularly so that it continues to support your needs. Some people check their budgets weekly, while others check them monthly; there's no "right" way. The key is to stay aware and adjust as life evolves.

For example, let's say you originally budgeted for a gym membership, but after a few months, you barely use it. Instead of sticking to an old plan, you redirect that money toward something more useful—maybe saving for a weekend getaway or boosting your emergency fund.

The Truth About Budgeting

At the end of the day, budgeting isn't about deprivation—it's about freedom. It's about knowing where your money is going instead of wondering where it went and making intentional choices that bring you closer to your goals, instead of feeling like you're constantly playing catch-up.

Once you shift your mindset, budgeting stops feeling like a chore and starts feeling like an empowering tool. Whether you're just starting, managing a family's finances, or planning for the future, having a budget means *you're* in charge, not your bills, not your paycheck, and definitely not your expenses.

So if you've ever thought, *Budgeting isn't for me*—think again. It's for everyone. And once you give it a real shot, you might just find that it's one of the most freeing financial moves you'll ever make.

The Role of Budgeting in Financial Health

When you think about financial health, you might picture things like having a solid savings account, staying out of debt, or feeling confident about your money decisions. But how do you get there? That's where budgeting comes in. Whether you're trying to stay on top of everyday expenses, save for something important, or simply stop feeling like your money disappears too fast, budgeting gives you the structure to make it happen.

Your budget isn't just a spreadsheet or an app—it's a roadmap that helps you take control of your finances, reduce money stress, and set yourself up for a secure future. Let's break down the key ways budgeting plays a huge role in keeping your financial health in check.

Tracking Financial Progress

Have you ever reached the end of the month and wondered, *Where did all my money go?* We've all been there. Without tracking your finances, it's easy to overspend without even realizing it.

A budget gives you a clear picture of where your money is going, helping you:

- **Spot problem areas:** Maybe you're spending more on takeout than you thought.

- **Find ways to save:** Even small tweaks can add up over time.

- **Stay accountable:** When you see your progress, you're more likely to stick to your financial goals.

Tracking your spending helps you make adjustments that benefit you in the long run, without having to give up everything you love.

Prevent Financial Crises

Life is unpredictable—car repairs, medical bills, job changes, or home emergencies can happen when you least expect them. The last thing you want is to scramble for cash or rely on credit cards every time something unexpected pops up.

That's why budgeting isn't just about managing day-to-day expenses—it also helps you prepare for the unexpected. By setting aside a portion of your income for an emergency fund, you're creating a safety net that can keep financial stress at bay. You can do this by:

- **Planning ahead for known expenses:** Tucking aside funds for annual car maintenance or holiday shopping can help you stay on track with your budget.

- **Building an emergency cushion:** A few hundred dollars saved now can save you from relying on credit cards later.

- **Reducing stress and financial panic:** Knowing you're prepared makes a huge difference in how you handle life's surprises.

Think of it this way—having an emergency fund is like having an umbrella before it rains. It won't stop the storm, but it will keep you from getting soaked.

Promoting Savings

One of the biggest reasons people struggle with saving is that it often feels like an afterthought—whatever's left over at the end of the month goes into savings (if anything is left at all). But if you don't prioritize saving, it won't happen.

A budget flips this mindset by making savings a non-negotiable part of your plan, just like rent, groceries, or bills. Instead of waiting to see what's left, you decide upfront how much you'll save each month—whether that's for an emergency fund, a big purchase, or your future goals.

- **Treat savings like a bill:** Automatically transfer money into savings before you spend on extras.

- **Make it realistic:** Even if you start small, consistency is what builds financial security.

- **Turn it into a habit:** The more you do it, the easier it gets.

For example, imagine a young professional who sets a goal to save $200 a month before budgeting for anything else. Over a year, that's $2,400 saved, without feeling the stress of scrambling for money later.

By making savings part of your financial plan, rather than an afterthought, you're setting yourself up for long-term stability without feeling deprived.

Bringing It All Together

So far, we've broken down the basics of budgeting, what it means, why it matters, and how it plays a huge role in your financial well-being. We've tackled key concepts like understanding income, categorizing expenses, and making savings a priority, all of which help you take control of your finances instead of letting your money control you.

Now that you understand the core building blocks of budgeting, the next step is making it personal. In Chapter 2, we'll dive into how to create a budget that works for you, one that fits your lifestyle, your goals, and the financial realities you deal with every day. You'll learn how to assess your current financial situation, set realistic goals, and structure a budget that helps you feel in control rather than restricted.

Let's get started on building a personalized budget that works for you!

CHAPTER 2

Creating a Personalized Budget

A budget should fit your life, not the other way around. Whether you're figuring out how to cover everyday expenses, setting aside money for big goals, or trying to break free from financial stress, building a personalized budget puts you in control. And the best part? There's no single "right" way to budget—only the approach that works best for you.

In this chapter, we'll walk through the steps to create a budget that fits your needs. We'll start by looking at where your money comes from and where it's going. You'll learn how to categorize expenses, separate necessities from extras, and set clear priorities so your financial decisions align with what matters most. We'll also explore innovative ways to tackle debt without sacrificing flexibility, as well as strategies to track spending habits and spot opportunities to save.

By the end of this chapter, you'll have a practical, adaptable budget that grows with you—one that helps you stay on top of your finances. The goal isn't just to put numbers on a spreadsheet; it's to give you confidence and freedom in your financial choices.

Assessing Your Financial Situation

Before you can build a budget that works for you, you need a clear picture of where you stand financially. Think of it like mapping out a road trip. Before you can figure out where you're going, you have to know where you are. Taking a close look at your income, expenses, debts, and spending habits will give you the foundation to make informed choices, plan ahead, and set financial goals that actually make sense for your life.

Understanding Your Income Sources

First, let's look at the money coming in. Your salary may be your primary source of income, but don't forget about other streams— side gigs, freelance work, rental income, dividends from investments, or even interest from savings accounts. If your income varies from month to month, perhaps because you're a freelancer or work on commission, understanding these fluctuations is even more important.

Listing all your income sources gives you a realistic picture of what's available. It also helps you plan for slower months and take advantage of extra income when it comes in. If you know a big bonus or tax refund is coming, you can decide now how to use it wisely rather than letting it disappear into mindless spending.

Identifying Fixed and Variable Expenses

Now that you know how much money is coming in, the next step is figuring out where it's going. Expenses fall into two categories:

- **Fixed expenses:** These are the non-negotiables, rent or mortgage, insurance, car payments, student loans, and utilities. They stay about the same each month and are usually the first things you budget for.

- **Variable expenses:** These change from month to month and often include things like dining out, entertainment, shopping, and travel. Since they're more flexible, they're the first place to look when you need to cut back or adjust spending.

Breaking expenses down into these categories makes it easier to identify areas where you can make adjustments. If you're looking to save money, cutting back on fixed costs might not be an option; you can't exactly call your landlord and negotiate your rent. But variable expenses? That's where small, intentional changes can add up fast.

For example, if you notice that you're spending a little too much on takeout, you don't have to eliminate it completely; maybe you set a goal to cook at home one extra night a week. These little tweaks can free up cash for bigger priorities without making you feel like you're depriving yourself.

Evaluating Financial Obligations (Debt and Recurring Payments)

Debt can feel overwhelming, but the best way to take control of it is to face it head-on. Start by listing everything you owe—credit cards, student loans, car loans, or any personal loans. Include the interest rates, monthly payments, and due dates.

Once you have it all in front of you, you can make a game plan. High-interest debts, like credit cards, should typically be tackled first because they cost you the most over time. Even small extra payments on these balances can make a big difference.

If your debt feels unmanageable, don't panic—there are options. Consolidation, refinancing, or even negotiating with lenders can help make repayments more manageable. The key is to stay proactive, so your debt doesn't control your budget.

Reviewing Financial Statements (Tracking Where Your Money Goes)

Now comes one of the most eye-opening steps—going through your bank statements, credit card bills, and receipts to see exactly where your money is going. This step might surprise you. Maybe you don't realize how much those small, everyday purchases—like coffee runs or streaming subscriptions—add up over a month.

Tracking your spending isn't about guilt—it's about awareness. When you know where your money is going, you can decide if it's going where you want it to.

Here's how to make it easier:

- Use budgeting apps that automatically categorize your spending. Apps like Mint, YNAB (You Need a Budget), or even built-in bank features can give you clear insights without all the manual work.

- If you prefer a hands-on approach, try the highlighter method: print out your bank statement and highlight spending in different colors (green for essentials, red for unnecessary splurges, blue for savings, etc.). Seeing it all laid out makes it easy to spot areas to adjust.

- Set a monthly money check-in to go over your finances. Even 10 minutes of reviewing can help you stay on track and catch any red flags before they become problems.

Setting Realistic Financial Goals

Have you ever set a financial goal that felt impossible to reach? Maybe you planned to save more, pay off debt faster, or finally build that emergency fund—only to feel discouraged when life got in the way. You're not alone. The problem isn't that your goals were bad; it's that they weren't set in a way that made them realistic and achievable.

That's where smart financial goal-setting comes in. A well-structured goal is a roadmap that keeps you focused, motivated, and on track. Without clear goals, even the best budget can drift off course, making it harder to see progress and stay committed.

SMART Goals Framework

One of the best ways to set goals you can achieve is by using the SMART criteria:

- **Specific:** Clearly define what you want to accomplish.

- **Measurable:** Have a way to track progress.

- **Attainable:** Make sure it's realistic for your situation.

- **Relevant:** Ensure it aligns with your priorities.

- **Time-bound:** Set a deadline.

For example, let's say you want to save for a vacation. A vague goal might be:

"I want to save money for a trip."

But a SMART goal would be:

"I will save $1,200 for a summer vacation by putting aside $100 per month over the next 12 months."

See the difference? This goal is clear, trackable, and realistic. It also has a deadline, so you know exactly how long you have to reach it.

The beauty of SMART goals is that they remove the guesswork. Whether you're saving for a down payment on a house, paying off student loans, or building an emergency fund, using this structure gives you a step-by-step plan instead of just wishful thinking.

Short-term vs. Long-term Goals

Not all financial goals are the same. Some are quick wins, while others take years to accomplish. Knowing the difference helps you prioritize and stay motivated.

- **Short-term goals (1 year or less):** These are things like building an emergency fund, paying off a small credit card balance, or saving for a holiday gift fund. Short-term goals are great because they give you fast results, which keeps you encouraged and moving forward.

- **Long-term goals (5+ years):** These include buying a home, saving for retirement, or paying off a mortgage. Since these take more time, breaking them into smaller milestones can make them feel more manageable.

Think of it like training for a marathon. If your ultimate goal is to run 26 miles, you don't just lace up your shoes and go—you set smaller milestones along the way. The same goes for your finances.

If your long-term goal is to retire comfortably, your short-term steps might include:

- opening a retirement account

- increasing contributions gradually

- learning about investment options

By combining short-term wins with long-term planning, you create a financial strategy that's both achievable and motivating.

Aligning Goals With Your Values

Ever wonder why some financial goals feel easier to stick to than others? It's usually because they're connected to something that truly matters to you.

For example, if education is important to you, saving for professional courses or your child's college fund will feel more meaningful than saving for a new gadget. If financial security is a priority, building a solid emergency fund might feel more rewarding than spending on impulse purchases.

To make sure your goals align with what's important to you, ask yourself:

- Why do I want to reach this goal?

- How will achieving this goal improve my life?

- Does this goal reflect what I truly value?

When your goals match your values, saving money stops feeling like a sacrifice and starts feeling like an investment in your happiness and future.

Reevaluating Your Goals Over Time

Life isn't static, and your finances shouldn't be either. A goal that made sense last year might not fit your situation today, making regular check-ins essential.

Here's how to keep your financial goals fresh and relevant:

- **Review them every 6–12 months:** Are they still realistic? Do they need adjusting?

- **Make changes when life changes:** A new job, a baby, or unexpected expenses might shift your priorities.

- **Celebrate progress:** Even if you haven't reached your goal yet, recognizing small wins keeps you motivated.

For example, let's say you're saving for a home down payment, but housing prices suddenly spike. Instead of feeling frustrated, you adjust, maybe you extend your timeline, explore different locations, or look into alternative housing options. The key is to stay flexible while keeping your overall vision in mind.

Tracking Income and Expenses

Building a strong, personalized budget is about staying aware of where your money is going. Keeping track of your income and expenses is what keeps your budget working for you, helping you make smart financial choices that align with your goals. By setting up a simple, consistent system to monitor your finances, you gain a clearer understanding of your spending habits, allowing you to adjust and stay in control.

Creating a Tracking System

At first, tracking every dollar might seem overwhelming, but it's one of the most powerful steps you can take toward financial freedom. Start by listing all your income sources—your salary, side gigs, freelance work, rental income, or any other money coming in. Then, categorize your expenses into two main groups:

- **Fixed expenses**: These are the non-negotiable costs, such as rent or mortgage, insurance, and loan payments. They don't change much from month to month, so they're easy to plan for.

- **Variable expenses:** These fluctuate based on lifestyle choices, such as dining out, entertainment, or shopping. These categories often hold the key to adjusting spending when you need to save more.

Once you have everything written down, patterns will start to emerge. You might notice that you're spending more on subscriptions than you realized, or that small, frequent purchases are adding up. Seeing where your money is actually going is the first step toward making intentional financial decisions.

Daily Check-Ins: A Simple Habit That Pays Off

One of the best habits you can develop is spending just five minutes a day reviewing your finances. A quick glance at your bank transactions can help you spot mistakes, avoid overdrafts, and make sure you're still on track with your budget. It's like checking the fuel gauge in your car; you don't want to wait until you're stranded to realize you're out of gas.

Daily check-ins also help curb impulsive spending. When you see how much you've already spent on dining out this month, you might think twice before ordering takeout again. Small, mindful moments like these add up over time.

Analyzing Monthly Spending Patterns

While daily tracking keeps you aware, looking at your spending on a monthly basis gives you a bigger-picture view. At the end of each month, take time to go over your transactions and ask yourself:

- *Are there spending categories where I consistently go over budget?*

- *Am I allocating enough to savings and debt repayment?*

- *Have I made progress toward my financial goals this month?*

For example, if you notice you're regularly exceeding your entertainment budget, you might decide to swap a couple of nights out for more budget-friendly activities. Monthly reviews help you make adjustments that prevent financial stress later.

Adjusting the Budget to Lifestyle Changes

Life is full of changes, some exciting, some challenging, but all of them impact your finances in one way or another. Whether it's getting married, switching jobs, moving to a new city, or navigating a sudden income shift, your budget needs to keep up. A rigid, one-size-fits-all approach won't cut it; flexibility is key to maintaining financial stability as life evolves.

Recognizing Major Life Events

Big life moments come with equally big financial adjustments. Getting married, starting a new job, or relocating all bring changes to both income and expenses. Recognizing these shifts early helps you proactively tweak your budget instead of scrambling to adjust after the fact.

- Marriage often means merging finances, sharing expenses, and planning for future milestones like buying a home or starting a family. It's the perfect time to have open discussions about money habits, financial goals, and how to fairly split expenses.

- A job change, whether it comes with a salary increase, a pay cut, or different benefits, calls for a review of your spending and savings strategy.

- Moving to a new city affects everything from rent and utilities to commuting costs and lifestyle expenses. A higher cost of living might mean tightening specific categories, while a move to a more affordable area could free up funds for savings or investments.

The sooner you adjust your budget to reflect these shifts, the smoother the transition will be.

Adapting to Income Changes

Whether your income rises or falls, your budget should adjust accordingly. The key is to have a plan for both scenarios so you're never caught off guard.

- If your income increases, it's tempting to upgrade your lifestyle right away. Instead, consider allocating that extra money strategically—whether it's paying down debt faster, boosting your savings, or investing in your future.

- If your income drops, focus on essential expenses first. Reduce discretionary spending where possible, and if needed, reallocate funds from non-urgent categories.

Evaluating and Adjusting Expenses

Just as you'd get regular check-ups for your health, your budget also needs routine evaluations to stay in shape. Take a look at your spending patterns every month and ask yourself these questions:

- Are you constantly going over budget in certain areas? That might be a sign you need to adjust those categories or rethink spending habits.

- Are you regularly under budget? Consider increasing contributions to your savings or investment accounts.

Even minor adjustments—like switching to a high-yield savings account for money you don't need right away—can help optimize your finances while keeping funds accessible.

Staying Committed to Your Budget During Change

Adjusting your budget isn't just about numbers; it's about adopting the right habits and mindset to stay in control, no matter what life throws your way. Here are some ways to do this:

- Make budgeting a routine. Weekly financial check-ins can keep you accountable and help you stay on track with your goals.

- Shift your perspective. Instead of seeing budget adjustments as restrictions, think of them as wise financial choices that give you more control.

- Use technology to your advantage. Budgeting apps can help you track spending and automate reminders so that staying on top of your finances doesn't feel like a chore.

- Keep communication open. If you share expenses with a partner or family, discussing financial changes openly helps avoid misunderstandings and ensures that everyone is on the same page.

Real-Life Examples of Budget Adaptation

Let's say a young professional switches jobs and earns a higher salary. Instead of immediately increasing their spending, they adjust their budget to put more toward retirement savings or work toward a big goal like buying a home.

On the other hand, a family relying on freelance income might experience fluctuating earnings. Instead of panicking during slower months, they set up a flexible budget that allows them to cut back on non-essentials when needed and save extra during high-earning months.

These examples highlight why budgeting isn't about restriction; it's about adaptability and financial confidence. Life will always throw changes your way, but with the right mindset and budgeting strategy, you can navigate them smoothly without sacrificing your financial security.

Bringing It All Together

In this chapter, we tackled the essential steps to help you build a budget that fits your financial situation, goals, and daily reality.

The ultimate takeaway? Budgeting isn't about restriction—it's about empowerment. Whether you're a young professional looking to gain control, a family juggling expenses, or a student learning to manage finances, the strategies in this chapter can help you create a system that works for you. With the right approach, financial independence isn't just a goal—it's something you can actively build, step by step.

Next, we'll explore various budgeting methods, as not every approach works for everyone. The key is finding the right system that aligns with your lifestyle, making budgeting not only easier but also sustainable. Let's dive in!

CHAPTER 3

Popular Budgeting Methods

W hen it comes to managing money, there's no one-size-fits-all approach—and that's a good thing. Budgeting isn't about forcing yourself into a rigid structure; it's about finding a system that works for you. Whether you're trying to break free from paycheck-to-paycheck living, set aside money for your future, or simply get a clearer picture of where your money is going, having a budgeting method that fits your lifestyle makes all the difference.

In this chapter, we'll break down some of the most popular budgeting strategies so you can see which one aligns best with your financial situation and personality. Each of these methods comes with its own strengths and best-use scenarios; some work well for people with steady incomes, while others are better suited for those with fluctuating earnings. By understanding how they work and applying them to real-life situations, you'll be able to make an informed choice about which system helps you feel the most financially secure and confident.

Zero-Based Budgeting

When it comes to managing your money, have you ever felt like it just disappears before the month is even over? You get paid, cover a few bills, maybe treat yourself to something nice, and before you know it, you're wondering where it all went. That's where Zero-Based Budgeting comes in. This budgeting method makes sure that every dollar you earn is accounted for and given a job, so nothing goes to waste.

Instead of guessing or relying on past spending habits, Zero-Based Budgeting starts from scratch every month. That means you actively decide where your money should go—whether it's toward covering bills, building savings, or knocking out debt. It's a way to take complete control of your finances, ensuring that every dollar works for you, rather than slipping away unnoticed.

How Zero-Based Budgeting Works

The core idea behind Zero-Based Budgeting is simple: your income minus your expenses should equal zero. This doesn't mean you spend every penny you make; it means you allocate every dollar to a specific category. This lets you make sure that:

- Your fixed expenses (like rent or mortgage, utilities, and insurance) are covered.

- Your variable expenses (like groceries, entertainment, and shopping) are planned for.

- Your savings and debt repayment goals are built into the budget from the start.

- Any extra income is intentionally assigned, rather than spent impulsively.

With this approach, you're in charge of where your money goes. Nothing is left unaccounted for, which eliminates financial guesswork and prevents overspending.

How to Set Up a Zero-Based Budget

Starting a Zero-Based Budget might feel like a lot of effort at first, but once you get into the habit, it becomes second nature. Follow the steps below to set it up.

1. List Your Income Sources

Write down all the money you expect to receive for the month—this includes your salary, freelance work, side gigs, and even passive income like dividends or rental earnings. If your income fluctuates, estimate conservatively to avoid budgeting based on overly optimistic numbers.

2. Categorize Your Expenses

Break down your spending into three categories:

- **Fixed Expenses:** Rent/mortgage, car payments, insurance, and any other costs that stay the same each month.

- **Variable Expenses:** Groceries, dining out, transportation, entertainment, and anything that changes month to month.

- **Financial Goals:** Savings, investments, debt repayment, etc.

3. Assign Every Dollar a Job

Now, take your total income and allocate every dollar into one of the categories above. The goal is for your total income minus your expenses to equal zero.

For example, if you bring in $3,000 a month:

- $1,500 goes to fixed expenses

- $800 goes to variable expenses

- $500 goes to savings and debt repayment

- $200 is set aside for upcoming irregular expenses (like car maintenance or annual insurance payments)

By the time you've finished budgeting, every single dollar is accounted for.

4. Track and Adjust as Needed

A Zero-Based Budget is only effective if you're actively tracking where your money is going. Check in weekly to make sure you're sticking to your plan. If an unexpected cost comes up, adjust your budget accordingly. The flexibility of this system allows you to shift money from one category to another, but you must always balance it out to ensure nothing is left unplanned.

Common Challenges With Zero-Based Budgeting (and How to Overcome Them)

Like any budgeting method, Zero-Based Budgeting has its challenges. The good news? Most of them can be easily overcome with a bit of planning.

- **Forgetting Irregular Expenses:** It's easy to budget for monthly bills, but forget about expenses that don't come up regularly, like annual car registration fees or holiday shopping. Solution? Set up sinking funds! Allocate a small amount each month toward these costs, so that when they pop up, you're prepared.

- **It Feels Too Rigid:** Some people worry that having to allocate every dollar means they lose flexibility. But in reality, Zero-Based Budgeting helps you gain control, not lose it. If you want to assign a category for "fun money," do it! As long as your spending is intentional, you're still following the system.

- **Takes Time to Set Up:** It might take a month or two to get the hang of it, but once you create a system that works for you, maintaining a Zero-Based Budget takes only a few minutes a day. Using budgeting apps or spreadsheets can speed up the process.

Who Should Use Zero-Based Budgeting?

Zero-Based Budgeting isn't for everyone, but it's an excellent method if you:

- Want to gain full control over your spending.

- Have a fluctuating income and need a flexible budgeting system.

- Are working on paying off debt or building savings.

- Need a structured plan to avoid unnecessary expenses.

Is Zero-Based Budgeting Right for You?

Zero-Based Budgeting is one of the most powerful ways to ensure your money is working in the best way possible. It eliminates guesswork, creates accountability, and forces you to be intentional about every dollar you earn.

While it does require commitment and regular check-ins, the benefits far outweigh the effort. With a Zero-Based Budget, you're not just spending money—you're making strategic financial decisions that support your goals.

So, if you're ready to take control of your finances, give Zero-Based Budgeting a try. You might be surprised at how empowering it feels to know exactly where your money is going, every single month.

The 50/30/20 Rule

When it comes to managing money, complicated spreadsheets and rigid budgeting systems can feel overwhelming, especially if you're just starting out. That's why the 50/30/20 Rule has become a favorite among beginners. It's simple, easy to follow, and flexible enough to fit most financial situations.

At its core, this budgeting method divides your after-tax income into three broad categories:

- 50% for needs: Housing, groceries, transportation, and bills.

- 30% for wants: Dining out, entertainment, hobbies, and shopping.

- 20% for savings and debt repayment: Building financial security through emergency savings, retirement funds, and paying down debt.

By sticking to these proportions, you create a balanced approach to spending, covering necessities, enjoying life, and still making progress toward financial goals.

Breaking Down the 50/30/20 Rule

50%: Covering Your Needs First

Half of your income should go toward essentials—things you literally can't live without. These include:

- rent or mortgage payments

- utilities (electricity, water, internet)

- groceries

- health insurance

- minimum debt payments

- transportation (car payment, gas, or public transit)

The goal is to make sure these basics are always covered before anything else. If your needs exceed 50% of your income, you may need to adjust other spending areas or explore ways to increase your income.

30%: Enjoying Your Wants (Without the Guilt)

One of the most important aspects of budgeting is allowing yourself room for enjoyment. That's why 30% of your income is dedicated to things you enjoy, such as:

- dining out at restaurants

- streaming subscriptions, movies, and concerts

- shopping for clothes and gadgets

- travel and vacations

- gym memberships or hobbies

This category helps prevent the all-too-common problem of "budget burnout." If a budget feels too restrictive, it becomes harder to stick with. By allowing yourself some room to enjoy life, you're more likely to stay committed to long-term financial success.

20%: Building Your Financial Future

The last 20% goes toward long-term financial health, which includes:

- savings (emergency fund, big purchases, retirement)

- paying off debt (credit cards, student loans, car loans)

- investing in wealth-building opportunities

If you have high-interest debt, it's a good idea to prioritize debt repayment first before focusing too much on savings. Eliminating debt frees up more money in the long run, making future budgeting easier.

Is the 50/30/20 Rule Right for You?

The biggest advantage of this method is its simplicity. There's no need to track every single purchase; you just categorize spending into three broad areas. But like any budgeting method, it's not perfect for everyone.

Who It Works Well For:

- Beginners who need a straightforward, stress-free budgeting approach.

- Young professionals starting to earn a steady income.

- People with predictable expenses who can easily divide their spending.

- Anyone who wants a flexible budget that allows for fun while saving.

Who Might Need to Adjust It:

- **People in high-cost-of-living areas:** If rent alone takes up more than 50% of your budget, you may need to tweak the percentages.

- **Those with high debt:** If you're working aggressively to pay off loans, you may need to put more than 20% toward debt repayment.

- **Families with fluctuating incomes:** A more adaptable method may work better for households with seasonal work or variable earnings.

Customizing the Rule to Fit Your Life

If the standard 50/30/20 split doesn't quite fit your situation, don't stress. The key is adjusting the numbers to match your reality while keeping the basic structure in place.

- If you live in an expensive city, you might shift to 60/20/20 (60% needs, 20% wants, 20% savings).

- If you want to pay off debt faster, try 40/30/30 (40% needs, 30% wants, 30% savings/debt repayment).

- If you have a fluctuating income, you can adjust the percentages each month based on what you earn.

The goal isn't to stick to rigid numbers—it's to build a financial plan that works for you.

The Envelope Method

Managing your money can sometimes feel like a blur—swiping your card here, tapping your phone there, and before you know it, your bank balance looks nothing like what you expected. If you've ever wished for a more tangible way to keep your spending in check, the Envelope Method might be precisely what you need.

How It Works

The idea is simple: you divide your cash into physical envelopes, each labeled for a different spending category, groceries, gas, dining out, entertainment, and so on. Every time you make a purchase, you take the money from the corresponding envelope. Once the cash in that envelope is gone, you stop spending in that category for the month. No borrowing from other envelopes, no quick credit card swipes—just a clear, visual way to see where your money is going.

This method forces you to be intentional with your spending. When you physically hand over cash, you feel the money leaving your hands in a way that a tap of a card just can't replicate. It makes you more aware of your financial choices and helps curb impulse spending.

Getting Started

Setting up the Envelope Method is straightforward:

- **List Your Spending Categories:** Start with essentials like rent, utilities, and groceries. Then add discretionary categories like entertainment, dining out, or personal spending.

- **Decide How Much Goes into Each Envelope:** Use your budget to allocate cash to each category. If you've budgeted $300 for groceries, put exactly that amount into the "Groceries" envelope.

- **Stick to the Plan:** When an envelope runs out, that's it—no dipping into savings or borrowing from another category. This keeps your spending disciplined and intentional.

- **Track Your Spending:** Write amounts on the back of the envelope or keep a small notebook to track what's left. This helps you stay accountable throughout the month.

Modernizing the Envelope Method

Not everyone carries cash these days, but that doesn't mean this method is outdated. Many budgeting apps now offer a "digital envelope" system that mimics the traditional method while allowing you to keep using debit and credit cards. Apps like Goodbudget and Mvelopes let you assign money to digital categories, so you can still follow the same structure without handling physical cash.

If you tend to overspend with cards, though, sticking to real cash envelopes—even for just a few months—can be a great way to reset your spending habits before transitioning to a digital system.

Is This Method Right for You?

The Envelope Method works exceptionally well if you:

- Struggle with overspending or impulse purchases.

- Prefer a hands-on, visual way to track your money.

- Need a straightforward budgeting system without complicated spreadsheets.

- Need a structured way to stick to a spending plan.

However, it may not be the best fit if you rely heavily on online purchases or automated bill payments. In that case, a hybrid approach—using cash envelopes for discretionary spending while keeping fixed expenses digital—can offer the best of both worlds.

Bringing It All Together

In this chapter, we explored different budgeting methods, each offering its own way to bring clarity and control to your finances. Whether it's the structure of Zero-Based Budgeting, where every dollar has a job, the balanced simplicity of the 50/30/20 Rule, or the hands-on approach of the Envelope Method, these strategies give you a solid foundation to manage your money with intention.

There's no single "right" way to budget; what matters is finding the method (or combination of methods) that works best for you. If you need strict financial discipline, Zero-Based Budgeting might be your best fit. If you prefer a general structure that allows flexibility, the 50/30/20 Rule may be ideal. And if you need a concrete, visual way to curb spending, the Envelope Method can be helpful.

The most important thing? Stay adaptable. Life changes, and so should your budget. Whether you're dealing with an unpredictable income, working toward financial independence, or managing student loans, your budgeting approach should evolve with your needs. By understanding these methods and applying the one that fits your lifestyle, you're not just managing your money—you're taking charge of your financial future.

Up next, we'll explore financial tools and apps that can simplify the budgeting process, helping you stay on track with less effort. Let's dive into the technology that can make managing your money even easier.

CHAPTER 4

Financial Tools and Apps

M anaging your finances can feel overwhelming, especially with so many budgeting tools and apps out there promising to simplify the process. The good news? These digital resources really make a difference, helping you track your spending, set goals, and stay on top of your money without the hassle of manual calculations.

In this chapter, we'll explore some of the most popular budgeting apps and tools available today, breaking down what makes them effective and who they're best suited for. From apps like You Need a Budget (YNAB) that emphasize total financial control to Goodbudget, which brings an old-school envelope system into the digital world, each option has its own strengths. We'll also look at how spreadsheets, despite being a more traditional method, remain a powerful and highly customizable tool for personal budgeting. By the end of this chapter, you'll have a solid understanding of which financial tools can support your budgeting journey and how to use them in a way that makes sense for your lifestyle.

Top Budgeting Apps of the Year

Managing your money doesn't have to be a hassle, especially with the right budgeting app by your side. Whether you're looking for a detailed, hands-on approach or a simple system that runs in the background, there's a budgeting tool out there that can fit your lifestyle. Today's apps are designed to take the stress out of tracking expenses, setting goals, and staying on top of your finances—all in a way that works for you.

Best Budgeting Apps

With so many options available, three apps consistently stand out for their effectiveness in helping people manage their money: You Need a Budget (YNAB), Goodbudget, and EveryDollar. Each one takes a different approach, so the best choice depends on how you prefer to handle your budget.

- YNAB (You Need a Budget) is perfect if you want a Zero-Based Budgeting system, meaning every dollar you earn gets assigned a specific job—whether it's covering bills, going toward savings, or paying off debt. The app encourages you to plan ahead, spend intentionally, and avoid living paycheck to paycheck. It also offers goal-setting features and real-time syncing across multiple devices, so you can always keep your budget up to date.

- Goodbudget takes a digital spin on the envelope budgeting method, which involves dividing your income into spending categories (or "envelopes") like groceries, entertainment, and dining out. This system makes it easy to visualize where your money is going, which can help prevent overspending. A standout feature? Goodbudget allows families and couples to sync their budgets across multiple devices, making it an excellent option for those who share financial responsibilities.

- EveryDollar, created by financial expert Dave Ramsey, also follows a zero-based budgeting approach, but in a simplified, easy-to-use format. The app guides you through creating a budget step by step, making it a great choice for those new to budgeting or seeking a straightforward system. While the free version requires manual transaction entry, the premium version syncs directly with your bank account, saving time and making tracking effortless.

Budgeting Apps With a Unique Edge

While YNAB, Goodbudget, and EveryDollar cover the fundamentals of budgeting, some apps offer extra features tailored to specific needs:

- Honeydue is built for couples who want to manage their money together without feeling micromanaged. It allows both partners to track expenses, set savings goals, and keep an eye on shared bills without merging their bank accounts. You can choose what to share and what to keep private, making open financial communication easier while still maintaining independence.

- Monarch Money is ideal if you want a big-picture view of your financial health. It goes beyond basic budgeting by tracking spending habits, investments, and even net worth. If you prefer detailed reports and analytics to better understand where your money is going and how to make it work harder for you, this app is worth considering.

Why These Apps Make Budgeting Easier

Budgeting can feel like a hassle, but the right app can simplify the process and make it part of your routine. Beyond convenience, budgeting apps also help reduce the mental load of managing money. With built-in reminders, spending alerts, and visual breakdowns of where your cash is going, they take the guesswork out of budgeting. Instead of worrying about whether you've set enough aside for bills or overspent on dining out, you can rely on the app to keep you informed. Some even offer goal-setting features, helping you stay motivated by tracking progress toward savings milestones or debt repayment.

The best budgeting app is the one that fits into your life and helps you stick to your goals. Whether you prefer a structured approach or need a tool that works quietly in the background, these apps make it easier to manage your money, so you can focus on what really matters.

Using Spreadsheets for Budgeting

Budgeting apps might be popular, but sometimes, nothing beats the control and flexibility of a spreadsheet. If you want a completely customizable budgeting system—one that adapts to your unique financial situation—spreadsheets are an excellent option. Whether you're a young professional tracking multiple income streams, a family juggling shared expenses, or a student balancing tuition and daily costs, a spreadsheet can be designed to fit your needs exactly the way you want.

Building Your Own Budgeting Spreadsheet

One of the biggest advantages of using a spreadsheet over a budgeting app is that you're in charge of how it's structured. Instead of working with preset categories, you can create custom sections that reflect your actual spending habits. Have multiple side gigs? Track each income source separately. Want to see exactly how much you spend on fitness classes or pet care? Add those categories in. Your spreadsheet should reflect your life, not force you into a generic system.

If you're starting from scratch, you can either build your own spreadsheet or download a template that closely matches your financial goals. Most templates come with pre-set categories, but don't be afraid to tweak them to fit your spending patterns. The goal is to make sure every dollar is accounted for in a way that makes sense to you.

Unlocking Advanced Spreadsheet Features for Budgeting

Once you've set up a basic budgeting spreadsheet, you can take things a step further by using built-in formulas and features to automate tracking and make financial planning easier.

- Basic formulas can calculate totals, averages, and spending trends without you having to do the math manually.

- Conditional formatting can highlight overspending in certain categories, giving you a visual alert when you're going over budget.

- Pivot tables allow you to analyze spending trends over time so you can adjust your habits accordingly.

- Macros (for advanced users) can automate repetitive tasks, such as copying last month's budget into a new sheet or flagging unusual expenses.

Even if you're not a spreadsheet expert, these features can make tracking your finances easier and more intuitive, saving you time while helping you stay in control of your money.

Collaborating on Budgeting Spreadsheets

If you're sharing finances with a partner, roommate, or family member, a cloud-based spreadsheet (like Google Sheets) is a great way to stay on the same page financially. With real-time updates, both of you can edit and review the budget at any time, regardless of your location.

To make the most of a shared budgeting spreadsheet:

- Set up shared access so both people can edit and view changes instantly.

- Establish financial check-ins (weekly or monthly) to review spending, upcoming bills, and financial goals together.

- Use clear labeling and notes to avoid confusion. If one person adjusts the budget, the other should know why.

Having a shared system for tracking expenses makes it easier to manage joint finances, reducing stress and keeping everyone accountable.

Finding the Best Budgeting Spreadsheet Templates

Not sure where to start? There are plenty of free and premium spreadsheet templates available that can help kickstart your budgeting process. Microsoft Excel, Google Sheets, and platforms like Microsoft Create offer pre-built templates designed for different financial goals—whether you're managing a simple monthly budget, tracking savings for a big purchase, or balancing student expenses.

When choosing a template, look for one that:

- Has clearly defined income and expense sections, making it easy to track spending.

- Includes graphs or visual summaries to help you spot trends at a glance.

- Is easy to customize, allowing you to tweak it to match your financial needs.

Whether you prefer a minimalist layout or a more detailed spreadsheet with interactive features, finding the right template can make budgeting easier and more effective, without overwhelming you with unnecessary complexity.

Tracking Expenses Digitally

Keeping track of where your money goes each month is one of the most important steps in staying in control of your finances—and thanks to digital tools, it's easier than ever. Instead of manually writing down every expense, digital tracking apps do the work for you in real-time, ensuring you always have a clear picture of your spending habits.

Choosing the Right Digital Expense Tracking Tools

With so many expense-tracking tools available, selecting the right one depends on your specific financial needs and lifestyle. If you prefer a hands-off approach, apps like Mint automatically track your transactions and categorize them for you. This means that every time you make a purchase, whether it's groceries, rent, or a night out, the app automatically assigns it to the correct category without requiring any manual input. This automation eliminates guesswork and makes budgeting much easier.

For those who want more hands-on control, apps like YNAB (You Need A Budget) take a proactive approach. Instead of just tracking what you've already spent, YNAB encourages you to plan where your money should go before you spend it. This method is ideal for those who want to be more intentional with their budgeting rather than just reviewing past spending.

Regardless of which tool you choose, having an automated tracking system removes the stress of trying to remember every transaction and helps you spot patterns in your spending. Seeing exactly where your money is going makes it easier to adjust your budget, reduce unnecessary expenses, and stay on track with your financial goals.

Best Practices for Effective Expense Tracking

Even with the best tools, how you use them determines how much value you get. Here are some best practices to make sure you're getting the most out of digital expense tracking:

- **Check your app regularly:** Make it a habit to review your transactions at least once a week to ensure everything is categorized correctly.

- **Customize categories based on your lifestyle:** If you have unique expenses, such as gym memberships, subscriptions, or side gig income, adjust your tracking system to reflect your actual spending habits.

- **Use alerts and reminders:** Many apps allow you to set notifications for upcoming bills, low balances, or overspending in certain categories. These features help keep your finances on autopilot while avoiding surprises.

- **Review and adjust your budget:** Revisit your expense tracking regularly to see if your spending aligns with your financial goals and make adjustments as needed.

Integrating Expense Tracking With Budgeting Platforms

One of the most powerful features of digital expense tracking tools is their ability to integrate with budgeting platforms seamlessly. By linking your expense tracker to a budgeting app, you get a real-time, up-to-date picture of your financial health without needing to input data manually.

For example, YNAB integrates with bank accounts, ensuring that all transactions flow directly into your budgeting plan. This not only saves time but also prevents discrepancies between what you track and what you spend. If you're someone who wants full visibility and control over your financial future, this level of automation can be a game-changer.

Expense Tracking for Different Financial Goals

Many expense-tracking apps go beyond just categorizing spending—they also help you stay motivated by tracking your progress toward specific financial goals. Whether you're saving for a vacation, paying off debt, or building an emergency fund, many apps provide:

- Progress bars to visually track how close you are to reaching your goal.

- Spending limits to help you stay within budget for different categories.

- Trend analysis to highlight patterns and areas where you can cut back.

If you're someone who likes to see tangible progress, these features can be a powerful motivator to keep your financial goals top of mind.

Choosing the Right Tools for Your Needs

With so many budgeting apps, expense trackers, and financial planning platforms available, finding one that fits your lifestyle and financial goals is key. The best tool isn't necessarily the most advanced; it's the one that seamlessly integrates into your daily life and helps you stay on top of your finances without added stress.

Assessing Your Personal Financial Situation

Before jumping into any app or tool, take a moment to evaluate your financial habits and priorities. What are you hoping to achieve? Your choice of tool should reflect your personal needs.

- If you're saving for retirement, you might want an app that includes long-term investment tracking and goal setting.

- If you're a student juggling tuition, rent, and student loans, a tool that focuses on expense tracking and debt management might be more helpful.

- If you're part of a household managing a fluctuating income, you might need a platform that allows shared budgeting and real-time financial updates.

Taking stock of your financial situation before selecting a tool ensures that you're not just picking what's popular but choosing something that truly fits your needs.

Evaluating Tool Features Based on Your Needs

Not all financial tools are created equal, and some will be a better fit for you than others. When considering a budgeting app or expense tracker, here are some essential features to look for:

- **Ease of Use:** If a tool feels overly complicated, chances are you won't stick with it. Look for an intuitive interface that fits your comfort level.

- **Compatibility:** Can the tool sync with your bank accounts, credit cards, or investment accounts? Automatic tracking makes managing finances much smoother.

- **Customization:** Does the tool allow you to create categories and budgets that align with your lifestyle? A one-size-fits-all approach may not work for everyone.

- **Automation:** Features like bill reminders, auto-categorization of expenses, and progress tracking can save time and keep you accountable.

The goal is to find a tool that fits naturally into your routine, one that requires minimal effort to maintain but provides valuable insights into your financial health.

Testing Tools Before Making a Commitment

Before fully committing to a budgeting app or financial platform, take advantage of free trials and demos. Many apps offer a free trial period, allowing you to explore their features without paying upfront.

During this time:

- Use the tool daily to see if it aligns with how you spend and save.

- Test different features to determine whether they add value to your financial planning.

- Look for red flags, such as slow syncing, missing features, or overly complex navigation.

Trying out different tools before committing helps ensure that you're not just picking an app because it's well-reviewed but because it helps you stay organized and on track with your financial goals.

Staying Flexible and Adapting Over Time

Your financial needs won't stay the same forever, so neither should your tools. What works for you now might not be the best fit a few years down the road. Any major life events. Such events as getting married, switching careers, or buying a home can shift your financial priorities, and your budgeting system should adapt accordingly.

Make it a habit to evaluate your financial tools regularly. Ask yourself:

- *Is this tool still helping me stay on track?*

- *Do I need different features now than when I first started using it?*

- *Are there better alternatives available?*

Being willing to switch to a new tool or adjust how you use your current one ensures that your financial system remains relevant, practical, and tailored to your evolving lifestyle.

Summary and Reflections

Keeping track of your finances can feel overwhelming, but the right budgeting tools can make all the difference. The key takeaway? Your financial tools should fit your lifestyle and priorities. Choosing the right one starts with understanding your spending habits, financial goals, and preferred level of involvement.

However, remember that your financial needs will change over time, and so should your tools. Regularly evaluating and adjusting your budgeting system ensures it continues to support your evolving goals. The more engaged you are in your financial planning, the more confident and empowered you'll feel in navigating your path toward economic independence and long-term stability.

CHAPTER 5

Savings and Emergency Funds

S aving money is about creating financial security and peace of mind. No matter where you are in life—whether you're just starting your career, managing family expenses, or balancing education and part-time work—learning how to save effectively can be a game-changer. And while the concept of saving may seem straightforward, actually making it a consistent habit takes planning, discipline, and a bit of strategy.

Think about it, life throws curveballs all the time—unexpected medical bills, car repairs, or even a sudden job loss. Without a financial cushion, these moments can turn from stressful to overwhelming in an instant. That's why building a strong savings habit is so important. It's not just about preparing for the worst; it's about giving yourself options and reducing financial anxiety when the unexpected happens.

This chapter breaks down exactly how to approach saving in a way that works for your unique lifestyle and income. Whether you're aiming to create a financial safety net or just want to build better saving habits, this chapter will help you craft a savings strategy that's realistic, adaptable, and built to last.

Determining the Size of Your Emergency Fund

Having an emergency fund isn't just about putting money aside—it's about having the security and peace of mind to handle whatever life throws your way. Whether it's an unexpected medical bill, a sudden job loss, or an urgent car repair, having a financial safety net can mean the difference between a minor setback and a full-blown crisis. But how much should you save? The answer depends on your financial situation, lifestyle, and responsibilities.

Understanding Your Personal Needs

The first step in figuring out how much to save is taking an honest look at your monthly expenses. Start by listing out your essentials: rent or mortgage, utilities, groceries, insurance, and transportation costs. If you have loans, childcare costs, or medical expenses, be sure to factor those in as well. These are your non-negotiable costs—the things you need to keep your life running smoothly even if your income takes a temporary hit.

How Much Should You Save?

A common guideline is to aim for three to six months' worth of essential expenses. This gives you breathing room in case of a job loss or another major financial disruption. But this recommendation isn't one-size-fits-all—it should be adjusted based on your personal circumstances:

- If you have a stable income (such as a salaried position with strong job security), three months' worth of expenses may be enough.

- If your income is unpredictable (such as freelance or commission-based work), saving closer to six to nine months of expenses can provide a stronger safety net.

- If you have dependents (such as children or aging parents relying on you financially), aim for the higher end of the spectrum to cover unexpected expenses.

Take Jane, for example. She's a freelancer whose income varies from month to month. Because she doesn't have a steady paycheck, she builds up a larger emergency fund—closer to nine months' worth of expenses—so she's not stressed during slow work periods. On the other hand, Mark, a single parent, keeps extra funds set aside beyond the standard recommendation to prepare for unexpected childcare costs or medical needs.

Reevaluating and Adjusting Over Time

Your financial situation will evolve, so it's important to periodically review your emergency fund. Major life changes, getting a new job, getting married, having a child, or buying a home, can all impact how much you need to have saved.

For instance, if you're fresh out of college and renting an apartment, a smaller emergency fund may be enough to keep you covered. But as your responsibilities grow—maybe you take on a mortgage or start a family—you'll want to increase your savings to reflect those changes. The key is to adjust your fund as your life and financial priorities shift.

Automating Savings

Saving money is one of those things we all know we should do, but setting aside cash regularly can be a challenge. Life gets busy, unexpected expenses pop up, and before you know it, another month has passed without adding anything to your savings. That's why automating your savings comes in handy. By putting your savings on autopilot, you eliminate the guesswork from the process, ensuring that you consistently work toward your financial goals without having to think about it.

Setting Up Automatic Transfers

One of the easiest and most effective ways to automate your savings is by setting up automatic transfers from your checking account to a dedicated savings account. Many banks offer this feature, allowing you to schedule transfers on a weekly, biweekly, or monthly basis. The idea is simple: as soon as your paycheck hits your account, a set amount is moved into savings before you even have the chance to spend it.

For example, if you get paid every two weeks, you could schedule a $100 automatic transfer to your savings account on payday. This "out of sight, out of mind" approach helps you save consistently without feeling like you're making a big sacrifice. It's a small step that adds up over time, and before you know it, you'll have a growing safety net without the stress of remembering to move money manually.

Choosing the Right Account for Your Savings

After establishing automatic transfers, the crucial next step is to ensure your funds are actively generating returns for you. Parking your emergency fund in a high-yield savings account or money market account can help your savings grow faster than it would in a standard checking or low-interest savings account. These accounts offer higher interest rates, which means your money earns a little extra over time, all without any extra effort on your part.

Even if you're only able to set aside small amounts at first, the power of compound interest will help those savings accumulate. Over time, these regular deposits, combined with earned interest, can turn into a significant financial cushion. It's like giving your money a job— one that keeps adding to your security and peace of mind.

Using Apps and Technology to Boost Savings

Beyond automatic transfers, there are financial apps that make saving even easier—and sometimes even fun. Apps like Qapital and PocketGuard help automate savings by rounding up purchases or setting custom rules that trigger savings.

- Qapital lets you set up savings triggers based on your habits—like saving $5 every time you buy coffee or automatically transferring spare change from purchases into your savings.

- PocketGuard analyzes your spending habits and calculates how much you can safely save without impacting your day-to-day expenses.

These kinds of tools are great for anyone who wants to save without feeling the pinch. They integrate with your budget and spending patterns, helping you build savings effortlessly.

Reviewing Automation Strategy

While setting up automated savings is a great first step, it's not something you should just set and forget forever. Your financial situation will change; maybe you get a raise, take on new expenses, or shift your savings goals. That's why it's a good idea to review your savings plan at least once a year to see if adjustments are needed.

- If you get a raise, consider increasing your savings contribution before lifestyle inflation consumes that extra income.

- If your expenses increase unexpectedly, you may need to tweak your savings rate to stay on track without overextending yourself.

- If you're saving for a specific goal, like a down payment or vacation, you might adjust your strategy to meet your deadline faster.

Replenishing Used Funds Efficiently

After dipping into your emergency fund, the next important step is rebuilding it, so you're just as prepared for the next unexpected expense. While it might feel discouraging to see your savings take a hit, think of it this way: your emergency fund did its job. Now, the focus shifts to replenishing it efficiently so you don't find yourself unprepared the next time life throws you a financial curveball.

Creating a Replenishment Plan

Rebuilding your emergency fund doesn't have to feel overwhelming. The key is to have a structured plan with a realistic timeline. Start by determining how much you used and setting a goal for when you'd like to have it replenished. A typical timeframe is three to six months, depending on how much you need to save and what your current financial situation allows.

Breaking it down into smaller, manageable contributions helps keep you motivated. Instead of focusing on the full amount, set monthly or biweekly savings targets to help you stay on track. For example, if you need to replace $3,000 in your emergency fund within six months, aim to put aside $500 per month—or adjust based on what's feasible for your budget. Having a clear target makes it easier to track progress and stay committed to your goals.

Budgeting for Replenishment

The fastest way to rebuild savings is by prioritizing it in your budget. Just as paying bills or making loan payments is a non-negotiable financial goal, rebuilding your emergency fund should be a priority.

Take a close look at your current expenses and identify areas where you can temporarily cut back. Can you skip takeout for a month? Pause a few non-essential subscriptions? Minor adjustments like these can free up extra cash without making you feel deprived.

That said, balance is key—you don't want to completely neglect other financial priorities, like retirement savings or debt payments, in the process. A realistic approach might involve redirecting a portion of discretionary spending while still making steady contributions to other long-term goals.

Finding Extra Income to Speed Up the Process

If trimming your budget alone isn't enough, finding additional income sources can help speed up the process. Even small boosts in earnings can make a significant impact.

Consider:

- **Freelancing or Side Gigs:** Whether it's writing, graphic design, tutoring, or selling handmade crafts, a temporary side hustle can help accelerate savings. Platforms like Upwork, Fiverr, or TaskRabbit offer flexible options for freelancers.

- **Using Windfalls Wisely:** Tax refunds, work bonuses, or cash gifts can go directly into replenishing your emergency fund. Instead of treating unexpected income as spending money, use it to fast-track your savings goal.

- **Selling Unused Items:** Clearing out things you no longer need—whether it's electronics, clothing, or furniture—can generate quick cash while also decluttering your space.

The idea isn't to overwork yourself but to be strategic about boosting your savings when possible.

Avoiding Future Emergency Fund Use

One of the best ways to protect your emergency fund is by planning ahead for predictable expenses so you don't have to tap into it unnecessarily.

Think about the expenses that caught you off guard in the past. Were they true emergencies, or could they have been anticipated? Car repairs, annual insurance premiums, holiday gifts—these are common costs that tend to creep up unexpectedly.

To avoid using your emergency fund for things like this, set up dedicated savings accounts for predictable expenses. Setting aside a small amount each month for car maintenance or medical costs helps reduce the need to dip into emergency savings later.

If you've used your emergency fund in the past for non-urgent situations, take a moment to reflect on what happened. Could it have been avoided with better planning? Adjust your financial strategy so you're prepared for the next time a similar expense comes up.

Involving Your Household in Financial Goals

If you share finances with a partner or family members, talk about your financial goals together. Rebuilding an emergency fund is easier when everyone is on the same page.

Discuss simple ways to cut back as a team—maybe cooking more meals at home or pausing certain discretionary expenses for a few months. Small efforts from multiple people can make a big difference, and keeping open communication ensures that financial priorities remain aligned.

Staying Patient and Motivated

Replenishing an emergency fund takes time and consistency, so don't get discouraged if progress feels slow. The important thing is to keep moving forward—even small contributions add up.

Celebrate milestones along the way. If you set a six-month replenishment goal, acknowledge when you hit the halfway mark. These little wins reinforce good financial habits and keep you motivated to see it through.

Summary

Building an emergency fund is one of the most important steps you can take toward financial security. Throughout this chapter, we've explored what it takes to create a safety net that fits your unique financial situation. By determining the right size for your emergency fund, based on your monthly expenses and life circumstances, you can prepare for the unexpected—whether it's a job loss, a medical bill, or an urgent home repair.

At the heart of it all, having a strong emergency fund is about peace of mind. It's the confidence of knowing that no matter what happens, you have a financial cushion that lets you handle emergencies without panic or debt. By making saving a habit, staying adaptable, and using tools to simplify the process, you're building not just an emergency fund but a solid foundation for financial independence.

CHAPTER 6

Budgeting for
Different Job Situations

udgeting is about adapting to life's financial realities, especially when it comes to different job situations. Whether you're earning a steady paycheck, navigating the unpredictability of freelance income, or making a career transition, your financial strategy needs to match your employment situation. Having a clear plan not only helps you stay on top of your expenses but also puts you in control so you're prepared for the unexpected and set up for long-term success.

In this chapter, we'll dive into practical budgeting approaches for different job scenarios. If you have a stable salary, we'll explore how to track expenses, automate savings, and build financial resilience. Suppose you're a freelancer or rely on commission-based earnings. In that case, we'll break down how to manage fluctuating income, establish a baseline budget, and create a larger safety net to cushion against slow months. And if you're navigating a career shift—

whether it's a job loss, a transition to a new role, or a complete career change—we'll discuss strategic planning techniques to keep your finances steady, from reassessing your budget to investing in skill-building and preparing for income gaps.

No matter where you are in your career, the goal of this chapter is to help you build a budget that works with your financial reality, not against it. With the right strategies, you can adapt, remain financially secure, and continue working toward your larger financial goals, regardless of how your income changes over time.

Budgeting With a Fixed Salary

Budgeting when you have a steady paycheck may seem straightforward, but making the most of that income requires planning and discipline. With predictable earnings, you have the advantage of knowing exactly how much money is coming in each month—but without a solid plan, it's easy to overspend, miss savings opportunities, or be caught off guard by unexpected expenses. The key is building a budget that balances financial stability with long-term goals while still allowing room for flexibility.

Making the Most of Your Predictable Income

Since your paycheck arrives on a set schedule, your budget should be built around your fixed expenses first. Start by listing essentials, such as rent or mortgage, utilities, groceries, insurance, transportation, and any other recurring bills. These are non-negotiables and should always be accounted for before anything else.

Once you have those covered, you can look at the next layer of your financial plan: savings, debt repayment, and discretionary spending.

One of the best ways to make saving a habit without thinking about it is to set up automatic transfers from your checking account to a dedicated savings or investment account. Treat these savings like a bill you owe yourself, something that gets paid first, not just whatever is left over at the end of the month. This approach ensures that you're always making progress toward financial security without relying solely on willpower. If your paycheck is direct-deposited, check if your employer allows you to split your deposit between multiple accounts—this is an easy way to "pay yourself first" effortlessly.

Prioritizing Financial Goals Without Feeling Overwhelmed

Setting financial goals—like buying a home, building an emergency fund, or saving for a vacation—can feel overwhelming if you don't break them into smaller, manageable steps. Instead of just saying, "I need to save $10,000 for a down payment," break it down: "I'll set aside $200 per paycheck for the next 50 pay periods." This makes big goals feel achievable and allows you to track your progress more clearly.

A great way to stay motivated is to visualize your savings growth. Some people like using spreadsheets, apps, or even a simple chart to track their progress. Watching your savings increase—even in small increments—can help you stay on track and avoid the temptation to spend that money elsewhere.

Planning for the Unexpected Without Derailing Your Budget

Even with a fixed salary, life is unpredictable. Unexpected expenses are inevitable—whether it's medical bills, home repairs, car trouble, or anything in between, but they don't have to throw your finances off course. To avoid tapping into your savings or relying on credit cards, it's helpful to build a "miscellaneous" buffer into your budget. This is a small, flexible category for unexpected expenses that don't fit neatly into other budgeted areas.

Additionally, periodic budget check-ins are essential. Life changes. Your rent may increase, you might take on a new expense, or your goals may shift, so adjust your budget accordingly. A monthly review can help you see if your spending aligns with your financial priorities and make small tweaks before any problems arise.

Keeping Yourself Motivated and Making Budgeting Sustainable

Budgeting doesn't mean depriving yourself. Building in small rewards can help keep you on track. Celebrating small financial wins, like reaching a savings milestone or paying off a debt, can reinforce positive money habits. Your reward doesn't have to be extravagant, just something that keeps you motivated, whether it's a small purchase, a nice dinner, or a day off to relax.

Another smart way to get the most out of your fixed income is to maximize your savings. Consider using high-yield savings accounts, which offer better interest rates than traditional savings accounts. Some people also find it helpful to organize their savings into different "buckets" (such as an emergency fund, a travel fund, or a home repair fund) to keep everything clearly defined.

At the end of the day, successful budgeting isn't about restricting yourself—it's about giving yourself the freedom to live comfortably while building a financially secure future. When you create a plan that accounts for both your responsibilities and your goals, you can manage your money with confidence and make steady progress toward financial stability.

Budgeting With Freelance or Irregular Income

Budgeting when your income isn't predictable can feel like an uphill battle. Unlike a traditional paycheck that arrives like clockwork, freelance work, contract jobs, and commission-based roles often come with fluctuating earnings, inconsistent payment schedules, and financial uncertainty. But that doesn't mean you can't create a stable, well-structured budget—it just requires a different approach.

When you don't know exactly how much money will be coming in each month, the key is to plan for the lowest possible income scenario while making sure you're prepared for the ups and downs that come with an irregular paycheck.

Building a Budget With an Unpredictable Income

Setting a Baseline Budget

The first step in managing a variable income is determining your baseline budget—the minimum amount needed each month to cover essential expenses, even during slower work periods.

Start by listing your fixed costs, including:

- housing (rent or mortgage)

- utilities (electricity, water, internet, phone)

- insurance (health, car, renters/homeowners)

- loan payments (student loans, car loans, credit cards)

- groceries and other basic living expenses

This number becomes your financial safety net. Even if you have a month where your income is lower than expected, these essential expenses must be covered.

For example, if your minimum monthly expenses total $2,500, aim to keep at least that amount available at all times.

When you have months with higher earnings, be strategic with the extra income rather than spending it all at once.

Planning for Fluctuations: What to Do During High-Earning Months

Since income isn't always steady, use high-earning months wisely to prepare for leaner ones.

- **Save aggressively when income is high:** Set aside a portion of surplus earnings for future stability.

- **Build a larger-than-average emergency fund:** Unlike salaried workers with predictable pay, freelancers need a stronger financial cushion.

- **Avoid unnecessary splurging:** Financial discipline now prevents financial stress later.

For freelancers, it's often recommended to save more than the typical three to six months of expenses. Since work volume can fluctuate dramatically, setting aside at least six months' worth of living expenses in a high-yield savings account can help smooth out cash flow challenges.

For example, if your baseline expenses are $2,500 per month, saving $15,000 (six months of expenses) provides financial security during slow periods.

If that feels overwhelming, start with a smaller goal and build from there. Even saving one month's worth of expenses is a good start, and making saving a habit will help you increase that amount over time.

Where to Keep Your Savings for Maximum Benefit

Freelancers need quick access to their savings, but that doesn't mean money should sit in a low-interest checking account. High-yield savings accounts and money market accounts offer better interest rates, helping savings grow while keeping funds easily accessible.

If possible, consider dividing savings into different categories:

- **Short-term emergency fund:** Three to six months of expenses in a high-yield savings account.

- **Longer-term savings:** Additional funds in a money market account or certificate of deposit (CD).

- **Retirement savings:** Contributions to an IRA or other long-term investment accounts.

This approach ensures that money is available when needed while also benefiting from interest growth.

Managing Irregular Cash Flow Without Stress

Since freelancers don't always get paid on a set schedule, having a structured system for managing money can help create stability.

Strategies to maintain control include:

- **Use separate accounts:** Keeping personal and business finances separate makes it easier to track earnings and expenses.

- **Pay yourself a salary:** Instead of spending income as it arrives, transfer a set amount to a personal account each month.

- **Set aside money for taxes:** Freelancers are responsible for their own taxes, so automatically setting aside 25-30 percent of income prevents tax season surprises.

- **Use budgeting apps designed for freelancers:** Tools like YNAB, QuickBooks Self-Employed, and Wave can automate income tracking, expenses, and tax planning.

Avoiding Lifestyle Creep and Overspending

When a high-income month comes along, it's tempting to indulge in luxury purchases or spontaneous travel. While rewarding yourself is important, it's easy for a temporary income increase to lead to permanently higher spending habits.

One way to stay disciplined is to follow a set income allocation strategy, such as:

- Saving at least 50 percent of surplus income.

- Using 30 percent for business-related investments, such as tools, training, or marketing.

- Allocating 20 percent toward discretionary spending.

By prioritizing savings and strategic spending, you maintain financial security without feeling deprived.

Budgeting During Career Transitions

Career transitions, whether planned or unexpected, can feel overwhelming, both emotionally and financially. Whether you're switching jobs, exploring a new industry, or facing a period of unemployment, adjusting your budget can make all the difference in staying afloat and feeling in control. The key is adapting your financial plan to meet immediate needs while preparing for long-term success.

Budgeting for a Job Change

If you're considering a career move, take a proactive approach to your finances before making the leap. Begin by reviewing your current budget and identifying areas where you can reduce non-essential expenses. That might mean dining out less, pausing unnecessary subscriptions, or postponing large purchases.

The goal here isn't to deprive yourself, it's to free up as much financial flexibility as possible. A career transition often means dealing with income gaps, whether it's the time between jobs or the possibility of a lower starting salary in a new field.

One of the best ways to ease financial stress during a job transition is by having a strong emergency fund. Ideally, you should aim for at least three to six months' worth of living expenses in savings. This gives you breathing room while job hunting or adjusting to a new salary. If you're still employed but planning a change, start building this safety net now.

Investing in Your Future

Suppose your career transition involves switching industries, advancing to a new role, or learning new skills; set aside money for professional development. Investing in courses, certifications, or workshops can improve your chances of landing a better job while keeping you competitive in the job market.

Many affordable online platforms offer high-quality training at a fraction of the cost of traditional education. If you're currently working, consider whether your employer offers reimbursement for professional development. Even small investments in your skillset can pay off significantly in the long run.

Bridging the Income Gap

If there's a chance you might have time between jobs, it's a good idea to find alternative income sources to help smooth the transition. Freelancing, consulting, or part-time gig work can provide some stability while you search for a full-time position.

Think about your existing skills and how they can be leveraged for short-term opportunities. Whether it's writing, tutoring, graphic design, or even rideshare driving, side income can help cover essential expenses without dipping into savings too quickly.

Lastly, don't forget about essential coverages, such as health insurance. If your job provides health benefits, make sure you understand what happens if you leave, whether you need to switch to a spouse's plan, buy temporary insurance, or look for a job that offers immediate benefits? Maintaining healthcare coverage helps prevent costly surprises during an already uncertain time.

Budgeting During Unemployment

If you find yourself unemployed, a survival budget becomes your best tool for staying financially stable. This means prioritizing the necessary only:

- housing (rent/mortgage)

- food (groceries, not takeout)

- utilities (electricity, water, phone)

- healthcare (insurance, prescriptions)

For the time being, luxury expenses like entertainment, dining out, and shopping need to take a backseat.

Accessing Available Resources

If unemployment benefits are available, apply as soon as possible. Many government and community programs provide temporary assistance with job placement, food security, and housing support. If you're eligible, taking advantage of these resources can help you stretch your savings while looking for new opportunities.

Making a Plan for the Next Step

Even during unemployment, it's helpful to have a game plan for how you'll get back on track financially. When you land your next job, don't immediately return to old spending habits—instead, focus on:

- Rebuilding your emergency fund so you're better prepared for future changes.

- Reviewing what worked and what didn't in your financial approach. Did you underestimate your savings needs? Did a particular budgeting method help keep you afloat?

- Continuing professional development even after securing a new role, to ensure you remain competitive in your field.

Concluding Thoughts

One of the biggest financial challenges we face is learning to budget effectively, regardless of how our income fluctuates. Whether you're working with a stable paycheck, managing unpredictable freelance earnings, or going through a career transition, having a flexible approach to budgeting can help you stay in control.

No matter what stage of employment you're in, budgeting is about more than just numbers—it's about creating a system that supports your long-term financial security and personal goals. By consistently reviewing your budget, making adjustments in response to life changes, and staying proactive about saving, you can build financial resilience and stay on track, regardless of where your career takes you.

CHAPTER 7

Debt Elimination Strategies

D ebt can feel like a weight that holds you back from financial freedom, but eliminating it is more than just a monetary goal. It's a life-changing step toward stability and peace of mind. Whether you're dealing with student loans, credit card balances, or other financial obligations, having a plan to tackle debt can help you move forward with confidence.

In this chapter, we'll explore proven debt elimination strategies, including the Snowball and Avalanche methods. These approaches help break down large, intimidating debts into manageable steps, allowing you to track your progress and stay motivated along the way. You'll also learn how to prioritize which debts to tackle first, avoid common pitfalls, and celebrate small wins that will keep you going. The goal is not just to get rid of debt—it's to give yourself the financial freedom to focus on what truly matters, without debt hanging over you.

The Debt Snowball Approach

How the Debt Snowball Method Works

Think of rolling a snowball down a hill. It starts small, but as it moves forward, it accumulates more snow, gaining momentum and growing larger. The Debt Snowball Method works the same way— by starting small, gaining confidence, and using that momentum to tackle bigger debts one by one.

This method is built on motivation and achieving quick wins rather than adhering to strict mathematical efficiency. Instead of worrying about interest rates right away, you focus on paying off your smallest debt first. Seeing a balance go to zero gives you a mental boost, like crossing something off your to-do list. That satisfaction keeps you going, pushing you to tackle the next one. For young professionals trying to get ahead or students struggling with debt, these small wins make all the difference in staying motivated.

Step 1: List Your Debts

Before you can start crushing debt, you need to see the whole picture. Create a list of all your outstanding debts, ordered from the smallest to the largest balance, without considering interest rates yet.

Your list might look something like this:

Debt	Balance	Minimum Payment
Credit Card	$600	$25
Car Loan	$3,500	$150
Student Loan	$9,000	$100
Personal Loan	$12,000	$200

This step is crucial because it makes your debt tangible and more manageable. Instead of being overwhelmed by one big number, you see it broken down into manageable steps. Think of each debt as stepping stones across a river; you're just focusing on reaching the next one.

Step 2: Attack the Smallest Debt First

With your list in hand, the next step is to focus all your extra money on the smallest balance while still making minimum payments on the others. Even small amounts, an extra $20 or $50, make a difference.

Where do you find extra money?

- Cut back on non-essential spending (like takeout or subscriptions you don't use).

- Use bonuses, tax refunds, or side gig earnings to accelerate progress.

- Sell items you no longer need and use the money to pay off your smallest debt.

Once that first debt is completely paid off, take the amount you were paying on it and add it to the next debt on your list. If you were paying $25 toward your credit card and it's now gone, roll that $25 into your car loan payment. Suddenly, instead of $150, you're putting $175 toward that debt, helping it disappear faster.

Step 3: Celebrate Small Wins

Debt repayment can feel overwhelming, so celebrating milestones along the way is important. Each time you pay off a debt, take a moment to acknowledge it—even if it's just treating yourself to a small reward. It keeps you engaged and motivated to keep going.

You don't need a big celebration that sets you back financially, just something meaningful like:

- A nice homemade meal instead of dining out.

- A fun, free activity with friends.

- A quick coffee treat or a favorite snack.

The point is to make progress feel good, so you stay committed to the long-term goal.

Step 4: Build Momentum

As you keep paying off debts, the amount you have available to put toward the next one grows larger and larger. What started as a slow process soon picks up speed, like a snowball rolling downhill.

For example:

- You finish paying off your credit card ($600) → The $25 payment rolls into your car loan.

- You finish paying off your car loan ($3,500) → The $175 payment now goes toward your student loan.

- You finish paying off your student loan ($9,000) → Now you have $275 going to your loan.

This compounding effect is why the Snowball Method works so well. It turns small progress into big results over time.

Does the Debt Snowball Make Sense for You?

While this approach is great for motivation, it doesn't always result in the most cost-effective interest savings. If you want to minimize interest costs, the Debt Avalanche Method (which we'll discuss next) might be a better fit. But for people who need quick wins to stay committed, the Snowball Method is one of the most effective ways to stay on track and eliminate debt for good.

Whatever method you choose, the most important thing is to take action. The sooner you start, the faster you'll be free from debt—and that freedom is worth every effort.

The Avalanche Method

How the Avalanche Method Works

The Avalanche Method is a strategic way to pay off debt while minimizing the amount of interest you pay over time. Instead of focusing on debt balances, this method prioritizes the debts with the highest interest rates first, saving you money in the long run.

If you're someone who wants the most financially efficient way to eliminate debt, the Avalanche Method might be the best fit. It may not give the quick psychological wins of the Snowball Method, but it maximizes savings by attacking the debts that cost you the most.

Listing Debts by Interest Rate

Begin by listing all outstanding debts, meticulously noting the interest rate for each one. This step helps visualize which loans are most costly over time, often revealing that credit card balances, personal loans, and certain student loans tend to accumulate the highest levels of interest. By organizing debts based on these rates, you can pinpoint exactly where your repayment efforts should be concentrated.

Step 1: List Your Debts by Interest Rate

The first step in using the Avalanche Method is to organize your debts from highest to lowest interest rate. You're not focusing on balance amounts here—just the percentage you're paying in interest.

Your list might look like this:

Debt	Balance	Interest Rate	Minimum Payment
Credit Card	$4,000	22%	$100
Personal Loan	$7,500	15%	$250
Student Loan	$10,000	6%	$150
Car Loan	$12,000	4.5%	$275

This breakdown helps you see where your money is being drained the fastest. High-interest debts, like credit cards, can accumulate quickly if left unchecked. By tackling these first, you cut down on how much you're paying in interest, allowing you to put more of your hard-earned money toward actual debt repayment instead of interest fees.

Step 2: Focus All Extra Money on the Highest-Interest Debt

Once you have your list, your goal is simple: pay the minimum on all debts, but throw everything extra at the debt with the highest interest rate.

For example, let's say you find an extra $150 in your budget each month. Instead of spreading that money evenly across multiple debts, you put it all toward the debt with the highest interest rate first (in this case, the credit card). The faster you eliminate this high-interest balance, the less interest you'll have to pay over time.

Once that debt is gone, you roll the amount you were paying into the next highest-interest debt, increasing the payment size as you go.

Here's how it works in practice:

- You pay off your credit card ($4,000 at 22%) → Now, the extra money you were paying toward it goes toward your personal loan ($7,500 at 15%).

- You pay off the personal loan ($7,500 at 15%) → That money then shifts to your student loan ($10,000 at 6%).

- You keep this going until all your debts are gone.

Step 3: Stay Consistent and Flexible

One challenge of the Avalanche Method is that it can take longer to see progress compared to the Snowball Method, especially if your highest-interest debt also has the highest balance. It requires patience and commitment.

To stay on track:

- **Check your progress regularly:** Seeing the amount of interest you're avoiding can be just as motivating as seeing a balance disappear.

- **Be flexible:** If your financial situation changes, you might need to adjust your payment strategy. That's okay—the goal is to stay focused on reducing high-interest debt while keeping your budget realistic.

- **Celebrate milestones:** Even though this method is more numbers-driven, hitting key points (such as paying off a big chunk of principal) is still a huge achievement.

Why Choose the Avalanche Method?

The Avalanche Method is best suited for individuals who want to minimize interest and pay off debt as efficiently as possible. If you're motivated by saving money and can stick with a longer-term plan before seeing major victories, this method is a powerful way to take control of your debt.

Ultimately, the most effective debt repayment strategy is the one that keeps you committed and moving forward. Whether you choose the Avalanche or Snowball Method, the key is starting now, because every step you take brings you closer to financial freedom.

Prioritizing High-Interest Debts

Why High-Interest Debt Can Feel Like a Trap

High-interest debt is one of the biggest financial hurdles many people face. Whether it's credit card balances, payday loans, or high-interest personal loans, these debts can grow at an alarming rate, often much faster than people expect. The stress of watching a balance increase, even when making minimum payments, can leave you feeling stuck in a cycle that's hard to break. But the good news? Prioritizing these debts strategically can make a huge difference in how quickly you regain control over your finances.

How High-Interest Debt Grows So Quickly

The reason high-interest debt is so dangerous is the way interest compounds over time. With each billing cycle, interest is calculated based not only on the original loan amount but also on the accumulated interest from previous months. If you're only making minimum payments, you're barely chipping away at the principal, which means the debt continues to grow.

For example, let's say you have a $10,000 credit card balance at a 20% interest rate. If you only pay the minimum each month, it could take decades to pay off—and you'd likely end up paying thousands more in interest than the original debt itself. This is why making high-interest debt a top priority is one of the smartest financial moves you can make.

How to Prioritize High-Interest Debt Without Feeling Overwhelmed

- **Make a List of All Your Debts:** Write down everything you owe, along with the balance, interest rate, and minimum payment. Seeing everything in one place helps you make a plan.

- **Sort Debts by Interest Rate:** Organize them from highest to lowest. Credit cards and payday loans often have the highest rates, so they usually go to the top of the list.

- **Identify Any "Quick Wins:"** If there's a small debt that you can eliminate fast (even if it doesn't have the highest interest rate), consider paying it off first to get some early momentum.

- **Focus Extra Payments on the Highest-Interest Debt:** After covering minimum payments on all debts, throw everything extra at the highest-interest balance.

What Happens When a Debt Is Paid Off?

One of the best moments in personal finance is making the final payment on a debt. But what you do next is just as important. Instead of absorbing that money back into everyday spending, redirect those funds toward your next financial goal.

- If you still have debt remaining, roll the old payment into your next highest-interest balance to speed up the payoff process.

- If you're debt-free, redirect the payment amount into savings, investments, or retirement funds—using the same discipline that helped you eliminate debt to build wealth instead.

- If you've struggled with staying debt-free in the past, consider putting that money toward an emergency fund so that unexpected expenses don't push you back into borrowing.

Tackling high-interest debt requires a strategic approach, commitment, and patience. But once you gain control, you'll experience less stress, more financial freedom, and the ability to build the future you want, without the weight of debt holding you back.

Avoiding Debt Traps

Why Avoiding Debt Traps Matters

Getting out of debt is a financial achievement, but staying out of debt is just as important. The truth is, many people fall back into the same cycle, not because they lack discipline, but because debt traps are everywhere. Whether it's a credit card with "too good to be true" offers, a payday loan promising quick cash, or financing options that seem convenient but come with hidden fees, it's easy to get caught up without realizing it.

By recognizing these traps before they happen and putting safeguards in place, you can stay in control of your money and avoid slipping back into financial stress.

Recognizing Common Debt Traps

Debt traps are designed to look appealing. That's what makes them so dangerous. Some of the most common ones include:

- **Credit Cards With High-Interest Rates:** Many credit cards start with "0% APR" or low introductory rates, but once that period ends, the interest skyrockets. If you're carrying a balance, you could find yourself paying far more than expected.

- **Payday Loans & Quick-Fix Lending:** These loans target people who need fast cash, but they come with astronomically high interest rates and hidden fees. Even borrowing a small amount can lead to a cycle of debt that never ends.

- **Buy Now, Pay Later Plans:** While these plans seem harmless, missing payments can result in steep fees and damage to your credit score.

- **Unnecessary Financing Options:** Store credit cards, car loans with long repayment periods, and appliance financing deals can trick you into spending more than you planned.

How to Stay Ahead of Debt Traps

1. Budget for Future Expenses

One of the biggest reasons people rely on credit is that they aren't prepared for unexpected expenses. When you don't have savings set aside for things like car repairs, medical bills, or holiday shopping, credit can feel like the only option. That's why budgeting isn't just about tracking what you spend. It's about planning for what's ahead.

- **Break your budget into categories:** Separate your essentials (rent, utilities, groceries) from discretionary spending (dining out, entertainment).

- **Create sinking funds:** These are small, dedicated savings accounts for expenses you know are coming, like holiday gifts, annual memberships, or home maintenance.

- **Make savings automatic:** Even setting aside $25 a paycheck adds up over time.

By planning ahead, you won't feel pressured to borrow money for routine expenses, which keeps you out of debt in the long run.

2. Stay Informed About Financial Products

Debt traps aren't always obvious. Many come in the form of "helpful" financial products that seem like a good idea until you read the fine print. Before signing up for anything, ask yourself:

- *What are the interest rates, fees, and penalties*? If they're too high, walk away.

- *Will this help me in the long run*? Just because something seems convenient doesn't mean it's necessary.

- *Is there a better alternative*? Could you save up for the purchase instead? Could you negotiate a better deal?

Taking the time to do your research can protect you from making financial decisions that seem helpful but end up costing more than they're worth. Here are four key ones to watch out for:

- **Payday Loans and High-Interest Short-Term Loans:** These loans often carry extreme interest rates and short repayment terms, trapping borrowers in debt cycles. Instead, consider small-dollar loans from credit unions or employer-backed programs.

- **Buy Now, Pay Later (BNPL) Services:** While marketed as "interest-free," missed payments can lead to high fees and deferred interest. These services also encourage overspending and rarely help build credit. Paying in full or using a low-interest credit card is often the safer option.

- **High-APR Credit Cards:** Cards with interest rates of 20% or higher and hidden fees can make carrying a balance costly. Many also push balance transfers with hefty fees. Opt for a no-annual-fee, low-interest card and pay off the balance monthly to avoid debt.

- **Adjustable-Rate Mortgages (ARMs) & High-Fee Loans:** ARMs start with low rates but can spike unpredictably, making payments unaffordable. Look for fixed-rate mortgages with transparent terms to ensure stability and predictability.

3. Track Your Spending & Stay Vigilant

One of the best ways to avoid debt traps is to pay attention to where your money is going. When you're regularly tracking your expenses, you catch problems before they snowball: whether it's overspending, hidden fees, or fraud.

- Use budgeting apps or a simple spreadsheet to track your daily expenses.

- Review your bank statements monthly to check for any unexpected charges or subscriptions you may have forgotten about.

- Set spending limits for discretionary categories (such as entertainment, dining out, and shopping) to keep your financial goals on track.

Being mindful of how and where you spend helps you make informed decisions, ensuring you stay in control of your financial future.

Final Insights

Throughout this chapter, we've broken down some of the most effective strategies for tackling debt and how they can reshape your financial outlook. If you've ever felt overwhelmed by multiple debts, unsure of where to start, or frustrated by high-interest payments that seem never-ending, you're not alone. Debt can feel like a weight on your shoulders, but with the right approach, you can take back control and work toward a debt-free future.

The key to success in debt elimination is consistency. Becoming debt-free isn't just about numbers: it's about peace of mind, financial stability, and the freedom to make choices based on your goals rather than your obligations. Every step you take gets you closer to a future where your money works for you, not the other way around.

CHAPTER 8

Budgeting for Investments

Budgeting for investments involves a strategy to make room in your financial plan for long-term growth. It's not just about setting money aside but about prioritizing your future alongside your present needs.

In this chapter, we'll walk you through practical strategies for integrating investing into your budget, regardless of your current financial situation. You'll learn how to:

- Identify how much you can afford to invest each month, without sacrificing your everyday financial stability.

- Use clever budgeting techniques to stay on track with your goals while still enjoying your present lifestyle.

- Maximize the power of compound interest, so your money works for you over time.

- Understand the role of financial education in making confident investment decisions.

You don't need a huge salary or thousands of dollars to begin—just a willingness to prioritize your future and take small, steady steps toward financial growth.

Introduction to Investment Basics

If you've ever thought about investing but felt overwhelmed by the endless options and financial jargon, you're not alone. Many people hesitate to get started because they assume investing is complicated, risky, or only for the wealthy. However, the truth is that anyone can begin investing; it's just a matter of understanding the basics and making informed choices that align with your financial goals.

Types of Investments: Where Do You Start?

Think of investing like planting a garden. Different investments, like different plants, require varying amounts of care and patience. Some grow quickly, while others take years to flourish, and some are more resistant to bad weather. The key is knowing what you're planting and how it fits into your financial landscape.

Here's a breakdown of some of the most common types of investments:

- **Stocks:** When you buy stocks, you're essentially buying a small piece of a company. Stocks have the potential for high returns, but they can also be unpredictable. If the company performs well, your investment grows; if it struggles, so does the value of your stock. Some stocks also pay dividends, meaning you get a share of the company's profits regularly.

- **Bonds:** If stocks are about owning part of a company, bonds are about lending money. When you buy a bond, you're loaning money to a company or the government, and they pay you back with interest. Bonds are generally safer than stocks, but they also tend to offer lower returns.

- **Mutual Funds & ETFs:** These are great options if you don't want to pick individual stocks or bonds. Mutual funds pool money from many investors and are managed by professionals who spread the investment across multiple assets. ETFs (Exchange-Traded Funds) work similarly, but they trade on stock exchanges like individual stocks, making them more flexible and often less expensive.

- **Real Estate & REITs:** Real estate investing can provide both rental income and long-term appreciation in property value. If you don't want the hassle of managing property, Real Estate Investment Trusts (REITs) allow you to invest in real estate without actually buying buildings. REITs function similarly to stocks, offering dividends and long-term growth potential.

Investment Terminology: Making Sense of the Jargon

Before jumping into investing, get comfortable with some key terms:

- **Return on Investment (ROI):** This measures how much money you've gained (or lost) from an investment relative to how much you put in.

- **Capital Gains:** The profit you make when you sell an investment for more than you paid for it.

- **Dividends:** Regular payments some companies make to their shareholders as a share of their profits.

The Role of Time: Why Starting Early Matters

If there's one secret to successful investing, it's time. The sooner you start, the more your money can grow through compound interest, where you earn interest on both your original investment and the interest that investment has already earned.

Imagine you invest $1,000 at an annual return of 7%. In one year, you'll have $1,070. But in the second year, you'll earn interest on the full $1,070, not just the original $1,000. Over decades, this compounding effect can turn small, regular investments into a significant amount of wealth.

Linking Your Budget With Your Investment Goals

When you connect your budget to your investment goals, you create a system that ensures your money is working for you, not just covering daily expenses.

Making Investments a Priority in Your Budget

One of the biggest challenges in investing is consistency. It's easy to set investment goals, but putting money into those investments month after month requires planning. That's why setting aside a specific percentage of your income for investments, just like you would for rent, groceries, or savings, is one of the smartest moves you can make.

Even small contributions add up over time, thanks to the power of compound interest. Imagine putting just $50 a month into an investment account. It may not seem like much, but over the decades, that money grows significantly. By prioritizing investing as a regular expense, rather than something you only do when you have extra cash, you ensure that you're always building towards your financial future, regardless of life's ups and downs.

If your income fluctuates, like if you're a freelancer or work in sales, one approach is to set a minimum contribution amount based on your lowest expected income. When you earn more, you can contribute extra, but even in lower-income months, you're still making progress toward your goals.

Investing in Your Own Financial Knowledge

You don't need a finance degree to invest wisely, but taking time to learn about different investment strategies can help you make smarter decisions and avoid costly mistakes. Consider setting aside part of your budget for:

- online courses about investing and personal finance

- books by reputable financial experts

- subscriptions to trusted financial news sources

- webinars and podcasts that discuss market trends

Joining investment communities, whether online or in person, can also help you learn from others who have more experience. Engaging in these conversations can give you real-world insights into how different strategies play out, and you'll start to see investing as an ongoing learning process rather than a one-time decision.

Revisiting and Adjusting Your Investment Plan

Your financial situation isn't set in stone, and neither should your budget and investments. That's why it's essential to regularly check in on your progress and make adjustments as needed.

Maybe you've gotten a raise and can now invest more each month. Or perhaps a life change, like starting a family or buying a home, means you need to adjust your savings priorities. And sometimes, external factors, such as stock market fluctuations or economic shifts, can impact your investments, making it necessary to reevaluate your strategy.

Setting aside time, whether it's monthly, quarterly, or annually, to review your finances helps you stay on track and make informed adjustments. Review your investment performance, reassess your financial goals, and see if your current budget is helping you reach them.

Shifting Your Mindset: Investing as a Necessity, Not an Option

Many people think of investing as something you do if you have extra money left over at the end of the month. However, if you want to build long-term wealth, investing should be seen as a core financial responsibility, just like rent, bills, and savings.

A helpful approach is to categorize your expenses:

- **Needs:** Rent, utilities, food, insurance, etc.

- **Investments & Savings:** Contributions to retirement accounts, brokerage accounts, or other investment vehicles.

- **Wants:** Travel, entertainment, hobbies, etc.

By putting investments in the same category as essentials, you ensure that you're always prioritizing your future, even while managing your present.

Risk Management Strategies

Investing is an exciting way to grow wealth, but it always comes with some level of risk. Markets fluctuate, economic conditions shift, and even the most carefully chosen investments can experience downturns. The key to long-term financial success isn't avoiding risk altogether; it's learning how to manage it in a way that aligns with your goals and comfort level.

Assessing Your Personal Risk Tolerance

Before diving into investment decisions, it's essential to understand your own risk tolerance. Everyone has a different level of comfort when it comes to market ups and downs. Factors like age, income, financial goals, and personality all play a role in determining how much risk you can reasonably take on.

- If you're early in your career, you can handle more risk since you have time to recover from potential losses.

- If you're closer to retirement, protecting your investments becomes more important than chasing high returns.

- If you find yourself constantly worrying about market fluctuations, a more conservative approach may be better suited to your needs.

One way to gauge your comfort level with risk is to use risk assessment tools offered by financial institutions or investment apps. These tools ask questions about how you'd react in different market conditions and suggest an investment approach that fits your risk profile. Understanding where you stand allows you to invest with confidence rather than reacting emotionally to every market swing.

Diversification: The Ultimate Safety Net

One way to manage investment risk is through diversification. Instead of putting all your money into one stock, one industry, or one asset type, spread your investments across different areas so that a downturn in one doesn't wipe out your entire portfolio.

A diversified portfolio might include:

- **Stocks:** Higher potential returns but more volatility

- **Bonds:** Lower risk and steady income

- **Real Estate:** A tangible asset that often grows in value

- **Commodities (like gold or oil):** Protection against inflation

- **Exchange-Traded Funds (ETFs) or Mutual Funds:** A mix of investments in one fund for built-in diversification

This strategy helps protect against sudden downturns in any one market sector. If tech stocks take a hit, bonds or real estate holdings might help balance out the loss. By spreading your investments wisely, you reduce the impact of market volatility and create a more stable foundation for long-term financial growth.

Setting Up Protection Measures: Stop-Loss Orders

No investor wants to watch their investments drop in value, but market downturns are a natural part of investing. To protect yourself from major losses, consider setting up a stop-loss order on specific investments.

A stop-loss order is an automatic instruction to sell a stock or asset once it reaches a certain price. This helps prevent emotional decision-making; instead of panicking and selling everything during a market dip, your investments are protected with a pre-set exit strategy.

For example, if you buy a stock at $50 per share, you might set a stop-loss order at $40 to minimize potential losses. If the stock drops below $40, it automatically sells, preventing further losses. This kind of protection keeps you focused on long-term growth without the stress of constantly watching the market.

Adjusting Your Risk Strategy Over Time

Financial situations change, meaning your risk strategy should too. What worked for you five years ago may no longer align with your current lifestyle, income, or financial goals. That's why regularly reassessing your investments is crucial.

Major life events, such as getting married, having children, receiving a promotion, or preparing for retirement. This will require a shift in how you manage your investments. Similarly, economic changes, such as rising inflation or a stock market downturn, can impact risk levels in different asset classes.

Take the time, at least once a year, to review your portfolio and make any necessary adjustments. Ask yourself:

- *Am I still comfortable with my current level of risk?*

- *Are my investments aligned with my long-term goals?*

- *Do I need to rebalance my portfolio to maintain diversification?*

Staying proactive ensures that your investment strategy remains relevant, no matter where life takes you.

Creating a Diversified Investment Portfolio

Creating a well-diversified investment portfolio is one of the ways to manage risk and grow wealth over time. Instead of relying on a single investment type, diversification spreads your money across different assets, helping protect against market swings and ensuring long-term financial stability.

How to Allocate Your Investments Wisely

The key to a strong portfolio is allocating your investments across different asset classes based on your financial goals and risk tolerance.

- If you're young and have a long time until retirement, you might lean more heavily on stocks because you can afford to ride out market ups and downs.

- If you're nearing retirement, consider increasing your bond holdings and diversifying into lower-risk investments to protect your savings.

- If you have specific financial goals (buying a home, starting a business, or saving for college), you might mix different investments to match your timeline and needs.

One strategy to determine your ideal asset mix is the "100 minus age rule"—subtract your age from 100, and that percentage represents how much of your portfolio could be in stocks. For example, if you're 30 years old, a 70% stock and 30% bond split might work.

Balancing Different Investments

When selecting investments, consider how different assets complement each other. Some investments move in opposite directions. For example, stocks and bonds often have an inverse relationship (when stocks fall, bonds may rise). Having a mix of assets that behave differently helps create a steady portfolio that can handle market fluctuations.

For example:

- If you invest heavily in tech stocks and the tech sector crashes, your portfolio will take a big hit. But if you also own bonds or real estate, those assets may remain stable, helping to offset the loss.

- If inflation rises and reduces the value of cash savings, holding commodities like gold or real estate can help protect your purchasing power.

By thoughtfully selecting investments that don't always move in the same direction, you reduce the risk of major losses and create a smoother financial journey.

Rebalancing: Keeping Your Portfolio on Track

Over time, some investments will grow faster than others, causing your portfolio to drift from its original balance. If one investment becomes too large a portion of your portfolio, it can increase risk without you realizing it.

That's where rebalancing comes in. Every few months, review your portfolio and adjust as needed to maintain the right mix of investments. If stocks have grown too much, consider selling some and reinvesting in bonds or other asset classes to bring things back into balance.

Regular portfolio check-ins—whether quarterly, semi-annually, or annually—help keep your investments aligned with your goals.

Choosing the Right Investment Tools

Different types of investment vehicles can help you diversify efficiently:

- **Mutual Funds & ETFs (Exchange-Traded Funds):** These allow you to invest in a mix of stocks, bonds, or other assets with a single purchase, offering instant diversification. ETFs trade like stocks, giving you flexibility, while mutual funds are actively managed.

- **Index Funds:** A low-cost way to invest in an entire market index (like the S&P 500) without picking individual stocks.

- **Individual Stocks & Bonds:** While these offer more control, they require careful research and can be riskier than funds.

- **Real Estate Investment Trusts (REITs):** A way to invest in real estate without buying physical property, offering passive income through rental properties and commercial buildings.

For new investors, mutual funds and ETFs are excellent starting points since they automatically provide diversification. As you gain experience and confidence, you should explore adding individual stocks, bonds, or real estate investments to customize your portfolio.

Bringing It All Together

Investing isn't just about putting money into stocks or funds. It's about building a future where your financial security is in your hands. This chapter has demonstrated how budgeting and investing work together to bring long-term financial goals to reality. By setting aside even a small portion of your earnings for investments, you're not just saving, you're allowing your money to grow and work for you over time. Whether you're just getting started or already investing, making regular contributions, no matter how small, helps you take advantage of compounding, which can make a significant difference down the road.

The key takeaway? Investing isn't just for the wealthy or financially savvy. It's for anyone who wants to take control of their financial future. Over time, these small, intentional steps can lead to financial freedom and a future where you have the choices and security you've worked toward.

CHAPTER 9

Budgeting With the Family

Budgeting as a family is about building a life together where financial decisions support both shared goals and individual needs. When a family works as a team, a budget becomes more than just numbers on a page; it becomes a roadmap for making dreams a reality while ensuring everyday needs are met.

But money conversations aren't always easy. Differing spending habits, unexpected expenses, and shifting priorities can make financial planning feel overwhelming. That's why communication is at the heart of family budgeting. When everyone understands where their money is going and has a say in financial choices, it fosters trust, teamwork, and financial responsibility, essential life skills for children and adults alike.

This chapter will break down the process of family budgeting into manageable steps, helping you identify sources of income, categorize expenses, and create a flexible financial plan that adjusts to life's ups and downs. We'll also explore practical ways to manage money as a team, from holding regular family budget meetings to setting aside funds for unexpected costs. By the end of this chapter, you'll have a solid strategy to keep your family's finances on track while making room for both the practical and the fun parts of life.

Setting Shared Financial Goals

Discussing money as a family may not always feel natural, but when everybody is aligned about financial goals, it makes a world of difference. Instead of just making decisions in the moment, setting clear short-term and long-term financial goals together creates a shared vision, one that not only helps manage money wisely but also strengthens relationships along the way.

Bringing Everyone to the Table

The best place to start? A simple family conversation. Set aside time, perhaps over dinner or a weekend morning, to discuss what's important to everyone. Whether it's planning a summer trip, saving for a new home, or cutting back on unnecessary expenses, giving each family member a chance to share their perspective makes budgeting a team effort rather than a top-down decision. Even younger kids can participate, learning the value of money by contributing their own ideas and suggestions.

Aligning Short-Term and Long-Term Goals

Some goals bring immediate satisfaction, such as putting money aside for a family vacation, upgrading kitchen appliances, or budgeting for a fun night out once a month. These short-term goals keep things exciting and help everyone stay motivated. On the other hand, long-term financial goals, like saving for college, paying off debt, or investing in a future home, require more planning and patience. Having a mix of both keeps family budgeting realistic, balancing the fun things with responsible financial planning.

To stay organized, try using the SMART goals framework, setting goals that are Specific, Measurable, Achievable, Relevant, and Time-bound. Instead of saying, "Let's save for a house," break it down: "We'll save $300 a month for a down payment over the next three years." This makes the goal feel more realistic and achievable while giving everyone a way to track progress.

Making Sure Every Voice Is Heard

Not everyone in the family will have the same priorities, and that's okay. The key is to make sure that everyone feels heard, even if compromises need to be made. Perhaps one person wants to cut back on takeout to save money, while another feels strongly about occasionally treating themselves to a restaurant outing. The goal isn't to force everyone into a single financial mindset, but to find a balance that works for the entire household.

A great way to do this is by creating a family financial mission statement. A simple sentence or two that defines what's most important financially. Maybe it's "We prioritize saving for education and experiences over material things," or "We believe in living debt-free and setting aside money for emergencies." Having a shared financial mission keeps decision-making aligned with core family values, making it easier to stick to long-term plans even when unexpected expenses come up.

Tracking Progress Together

It's easy to set financial goals and forget about them, so visual reminders can help keep the whole family engaged. Consider a goal-tracking chart on the fridge or a shared budgeting app where everyone can see progress in real-time. Watching the savings for a trip, a new car, or a home deposit grow over time builds motivation and turns financial planning into something everyone can be excited about.

Of course, things change, budgets, priorities, and life itself. That's why you should check in regularly as a family. Maybe a job situation has shifted, or a new expense has come up. Adjustments are part of the process. Having regular, casual money conversations ensures that the budget remains realistic and flexible, making sure the whole family continues moving in the right direction together.

Building a Family Budget

The key to a successful family budget isn't about cutting out all the fun; it's about finding a balance between essential expenses, savings, and the things that bring joy to your family. With incomes that may fluctuate, varying spending habits, and unexpected costs popping up, it's essential to create a budget that's both structured and flexible.

Step 1: Understanding Your Household Income

Before planning how to spend and save, it's key to know exactly how much money is coming in. Families often have multiple income sources, including salaries, side gigs, government benefits, or even investment income.

For those with steady paychecks, budgeting can be relatively straightforward. However, if income varies from month to month, as is common with freelancers or commission-based work. It's best to budget based on the lowest expected income. This ensures that the family can always cover the essentials, even during slower months.

A simple way to do this is to track income over the past six months and average it to get a realistic estimate. If income is unpredictable, it's smart to build a cushion by setting aside extra earnings during high-income months to help during leaner ones.

Step 2: Breaking Down Expenses

Once income is clear, it's time to track where the money goes. Family expenses generally fall into two categories:

Fixed Expenses (Non-Negotiables)

These are the recurring costs that stay the same each month, including:

- rent or mortgage

- utilities (electricity, water, internet)

- insurance payments

- loan or debt repayments

- childcare or school tuition

These are the bills that must be paid, so they should be accounted for first before allocating money anywhere else.

Variable Expenses (Flexible Costs)

Unlike fixed expenses, these change from month to month. They include:

- groceries

- transportation (gas, public transit)

- entertainment (streaming services, eating out, hobbies)

- clothing and personal items

Because variable expenses can fluctuate, it's helpful to review past spending habits. Where is the family overspending? Are there areas where cutting back slightly wouldn't feel like a sacrifice?

Step 3: Planning for the Unexpected

Every family faces surprise expenses. A car suddenly needs repairs, a pet has a medical emergency, or school fees pop up unexpectedly. Instead of letting these costs throw the budget off track, set aside a small amount each month in an emergency fund.

Think of it like a safety net, one that keeps unexpected expenses from turning into financial crises. Even if it's just $20, $50, or $100 a month, every bit helps. The goal is to build a reserve of three to six months' worth of essential expenses, allowing the family to remain financially stable regardless of the circumstances.

Families with seasonal expenses, such as higher utility bills in winter or back-to-school costs, can plan ahead by setting aside a little each month to avoid large, one-time financial hits.

Step 4: Making It a Family Effort

A budget isn't just one person's responsibility. When the whole family is involved, everyone feels like they have a stake in the household's financial success.

Holding Monthly Budget Meetings

- Keep it casual—budget meetings don't need to be intimidating! Make it a relaxed conversation where everyone can contribute.

- Review spending—check where money was well spent and where adjustments can be made.

- Set new goals—whether it's saving for a trip, paying off debt faster, or adjusting your grocery spending. Small changes add up.

- Celebrate wins! Reached a savings milestone? Paid off a credit card? Recognizing progress keeps everyone motivated.

For families with kids, these meetings are a great way to teach financial responsibility. Even young children can learn about saving and spending wisely by helping set small family goals, like saving for a fun day out or a new toy.

Managing Household Expenses Together

Managing household expenses as a team is about creating a financial system that works for everyone. Families come in all shapes and sizes, and each household has its own way of managing money. The key is to find a fair and transparent approach that balances both shared responsibilities and individual spending.

When everyone understands their role in managing expenses, it creates less stress, fewer surprises, and a sense of teamwork in reaching financial goals.

Step 1: Defining Shared vs. Individual Expenses

The first step in managing household expenses together is getting clear on what's shared and what's personal.

- **Shared expenses:** These are the costs that benefit everyone in the household, such as rent/mortgage, utilities, groceries, insurance, and household maintenance.

- **Individual expenses:** These are personal choices, like hobbies, dining out with friends, subscriptions, or shopping for clothes.

A simple way to prevent conflicts is by setting clear boundaries on how much can be spent individually without affecting family goals. Some families set a monthly personal spending limit—a fixed amount each member can use however they like without guilt. This allows for freedom within structure, so that personal spending doesn't disrupt the household's broader financial picture.

Example: If each adult in the household has a $100 personal spending limit per month, they can use it however they want: a gym membership, a dinner out, or new books. This way, personal spending doesn't interfere with family necessities.

Step 2: Finding Smart Ways to Cut Costs Together

Even with a solid budget, reducing unnecessary costs frees up more money for savings and shared goals. A few simple habits can make a big difference:

● **Bulk Shopping for Essentials**

    ○ Buying in bulk lowers the cost per item and reduces last-minute expensive grocery runs.

    ○ Prioritize non-perishable or frequently used items, such as toilet paper, cleaning supplies, and pantry staples.

- **Meal Planning to Cut Grocery Waste**

  ○ A weekly meal plan helps avoid impulse grocery buys and wasted food.

  ○ Rotate favorite meals to balance variety and cost-effectiveness.

  ○ Include leftover nights to minimize food waste and maximize meal efficiency.

- **Energy-Saving Habits**

  ○ Switch to LED bulbs—they last longer and save on electricity.

  ○ Unplug appliances when not in use to avoid "phantom energy" costs.

  ○ Adjust the thermostat a few degrees to save on heating/cooling bills.

  ○ Encourage shorter showers and efficient laundry loads to cut water and energy expenses.

Family Challenge Idea: Set a monthly savings goal for utilities, and if the household meets it, use part of the savings for a family reward (like a fun outing or special meal).

Step 3: Assigning Financial Roles to Keep Things Running Smoothly

Managing household expenses works best when everyone has a role. Splitting financial responsibilities prevents one person from carrying the full burden and creates accountability for everyone.

Possible roles include:

- **Expense Tracker:** Keeps an eye on grocery, utility, and household spending.

- **Savings & Emergency Fund Manager:** Ensures a set amount is deposited into savings on a regular basis.

- **Bill Organizer:** Makes sure payments (rent, utilities, insurance) are made on time.

- **Budget Review Leader:** Leads monthly check-ins to adjust the family budget as needed.

Example: In a two-parent household, one partner might manage monthly bills while the other tracks savings goals. If kids are involved, they can take on small responsibilities, such as keeping a spending log of their allowance, to learn about budgeting.

For single-parent households, automating bill payments and using budgeting apps can simplify financial tracking without adding stress.

Teaching Financial Literacy to Kids

Teaching children about money gives them the confidence and independence to handle their future finances effectively. The earlier children learn about earning, saving, and spending wisely, the better equipped they'll be to make sound financial decisions as adults. Financial literacy isn't a one-time lesson—it's a gradual process that should evolve with them as they grow.

This section explores practical ways to introduce financial concepts at different ages, making learning fun, engaging, and relatable.

Step 1: Making Money Fun for Young Kids (Ages 4-8)

For younger children, money should feel like an exciting and interactive concept rather than an abstract or complicated one. The best way to introduce financial literacy at this stage is through play and hands-on activities.

Use Games to Teach the Basics:

- Board games like "Monopoly" or "The Game of Life" help children understand the concepts of earning, spending, and saving in a fun and engaging way.

- Pretend-play activities, such as running a store with play money, teach basic concepts like exchanging money for goods and giving change.

- A "Needs vs. Wants" activity, where children sort items into categories, helps them recognize the difference between things they need to live and things they want for enjoyment.

Introduce the Concept of Saving:

- A piggy bank or clear jars labeled "Save," "Spend," and "Give" provide a tangible way for children to separate and track their money.

- Parents can encourage saving by offering to match contributions, reinforcing the idea that savings grow over time.

- If a child wants a toy that costs $20, instead of buying it immediately, guide them through saving their allowance until they reach their goal. This teaches patience and the reward of financial discipline.

Step 2: Introducing Budgeting to Pre-Teens (Ages 9-12)

At this stage, children can begin to understand the importance of planning their money and making small financial decisions on their own.

Give Them a Simple Budget:

- Help them divide their allowance into three categories:

    - Savings (40 percent) for future goals like a bicycle or a school trip.

○ Spending (50 percent) for immediate purchases like snacks or small toys.

○ Giving (10 percent) for donations or gifts.

Involve Them in Family Budgeting:

- Show them real-life examples, such as how the family saves for vacations or unexpected expenses.

- Let them help make small financial decisions, such as choosing between a movie night or a home-cooked meal with a fun dessert.

- Introduce goal tracking through a chart or digital board where they can visually see their progress toward savings goals.

For example, if a child wants to save $100 for a skateboard, help them break down the goal into achievable steps. If they save $10 per week, they will reach their goal in 10 weeks. Seeing progress keeps them motivated and teaches them the value of delayed gratification.

Step 3: Preparing Teens for Real-World Financial Responsibility (Ages 13-18)

Teenagers are on the verge of financial independence, making this an ideal time to introduce real-world financial skills, such as credit, investing, and responsible spending.

Teach Them About Credit and Debt:

- Explain how credit cards work, including interest rates, and why paying off the full balance each month is helpful.

- Use examples to illustrate how purchasing a $500 phone on credit and making only the minimum payments can result in paying hundreds of extra dollars in interest.

- Consider giving them a prepaid debit card or a supervised credit card with a low limit to help them develop responsible spending habits.

Introduce Investing Basics:

- Explain the stock market in simple terms, such as how owning a stock means owning part of a company.

- Use a stock-tracking app or create a "mock portfolio" where they can follow companies and learn how investments fluctuate over time.

- Introduce the concept of compound interest, showing how even small investments can grow significantly over time.

Encourage Earning Their Own Money:

- A part-time job, freelance work, or a small side business, such as tutoring or lawn care, teaches responsibility and financial management.

- Help them set a goal for their first significant savings milestone, such as saving $1,000 for a future expense.

For example, if a teenager earns $300 a month from a weekend job, encourage them to:

- Save $150 for future goals.

- Spend $120 on personal items or entertainment.

- Donate $30 to a cause they care about.

This structure builds the habit of managing money wisely while maintaining financial balance.

Step 4: Teaching Smart Spending and Long-Term Habits

Regardless of age, helping children and teens build good spending habits will benefit them in the long run.

- **Encourage Price Comparisons:** Before purchasing an item, teach them to compare prices, check for sales, and consider alternatives.

- **Talk About Advertising and Impulse Buying:** Help them understand how marketing influences spending choices and why waiting before making big purchases prevents impulse buys they may regret.

- **Introduce Online Banking:** Once they are old enough, show them how to check their account balance, set up savings goals, and monitor spending digitally.

The most effective way to teach good financial habits is to model them. Children learn by watching how their parents handle money, so discussing family budgeting, making trade-offs, and saving for future goals demonstrates responsible financial behavior in action.

Bringing It All Together

A strong family budget is more than just numbers on a spreadsheet—it is a shared commitment to financial stability, responsibility, and future goals. This chapter has explored how families can work together to build a budget that balances collective aspirations with individual needs, ensuring that financial planning becomes a tool for unity rather than a source of stress.

Building and maintaining a family budget is an ongoing process that requires commitment, compromise, and communication. When families approach money as a shared responsibility, they create a financial system that is both stable and adaptable. With consistent effort, open discussions, and a willingness to adjust as needed, families can cultivate financial habits that provide security, growth, and peace of mind for generations to come.

CHAPTER 10

Budgeting for Retirement Planning

Budgeting for retirement is one of the main steps in financial planning, ensuring that you can maintain your lifestyle and financial independence in later years. While retirement may seem like a distant concern for young professionals or working families, starting early can make a significant difference in the amount you accumulate over time. The key is to integrate retirement savings into your budget just as you would with rent, utilities, or any other fixed expense.

By doing so, saving for retirement becomes second nature. A habit rather than an afterthought. With the proper planning, saving for retirement doesn't have to be overwhelming. It's about making steady, intentional contributions over time. This chapter will provide the tools and insights needed to build a sustainable and flexible financial plan for the future.

Understanding Retirement Goals

Visualizing Retirement Lifestyle

The first step in successful retirement planning is to clearly define what you want your post-work life to look like. Do you see yourself traveling extensively, moving to a quieter town, or dedicating time to hobbies and community involvement? The lifestyle you envision directly influences your financial needs, so the more specific you can be, the better prepared you will be to plan accordingly.

One primary consideration is where you plan to live. Some retirees prefer to downsize to a smaller home to reduce costs and simplify their lives, while others consider relocating to a lower-cost area or even moving abroad. Each of these choices carries significant financial implications, including differences in real estate prices, taxes, healthcare access, and overall cost of living. Factoring in these variables early allows you to create a budget that aligns with both your financial resources and personal aspirations.

Determining Financial Needs

Once you have a vision for your retirement, the next step is calculating how much you'll need to support your desired lifestyle. Start by estimating your potential expenses, including:

- housing (mortgage, rent, property taxes, maintenance)
- utilities and everyday living costs

- healthcare expenses (insurance premiums, prescriptions, long-term care)

- food, transportation, and entertainment

- travel and leisure activities

- charitable giving or family support

It's important to project these expenses realistically, keeping in mind that inflation will affect your purchasing power over time. A standard guideline is to assume a 4-5% annual increase in expenses due to inflation, ensuring your savings can sustain you in later years.

Healthcare is often one of the biggest—and most unpredictable—costs in retirement. While Medicare covers some expenses, it doesn't pay for long-term care, dental work, or vision and hearing aids. Setting aside funds for medical expenses or purchasing long-term care insurance early can provide financial security. Policies with inflation protection ensure that your coverage remains adequate as healthcare costs rise.

Another crucial component of your financial plan is creating a solid emergency fund specifically for retirement. Many financial experts recommend setting aside at least three to six months' worth of living expenses to cover unexpected medical bills, home repairs, or other emergencies without having to dip into long-term savings or investments at an inopportune time.

Strategic Income Planning for Retirement

A well-thought-out retirement plan includes multiple income sources to ensure stability. Common sources include:

- Social Security benefits (delaying benefits can increase payouts)

- Employer-sponsored retirement plans (such as 401(k) or 403(b) accounts)

- Individual retirement accounts (IRAs)

- Pension plans, if available

- Personal investments (stocks, bonds, rental properties, annuities, etc.)

Diversifying your income sources helps mitigate risk and provides financial flexibility. Understanding withdrawal strategies, such as the 4% rule. This suggests withdrawing 4% of your savings annually to maintain a steady income to help prevent prematurely depleting your funds.

Additionally, tax-efficient strategies play a critical role in maximizing retirement savings. Being aware of Required Minimum Distributions (RMDs), tax implications on withdrawals, and estate planning laws ensures that your retirement income is optimized and protected.

Incorporating Retirement Savings Into Your Budget

Planning for retirement isn't something to put off for later—it's a financial priority that should be built into your budget just like any other essential expense. The key is to integrate retirement savings into your overall budget in a way that is both sustainable and flexible, ensuring you continue to make progress while also balancing present-day financial responsibilities.

Prioritizing Retirement Contributions

One of the best ways to stay on track with retirement savings is to treat it as a non-negotiable expense, much like your rent or mortgage payment. This approach creates consistency, making it easier to reach long-term financial goals. Automating contributions is an effective way to ensure savings remain a priority—setting up direct transfers from your paycheck or bank account into a retirement account removes the temptation to skip a month or spend the money elsewhere.

A widely recommended savings target is 15% of your pre-tax income. If that seems overwhelming, start where you can and increase your contributions gradually, particularly when you receive raises or bonuses. Many employer-sponsored retirement plans, such as 401(k)s, offer automatic contribution increases, which can help you build savings with minimal effort.

If your employer offers a 401(k) match, make sure to contribute enough to take full advantage of it. Employer-matching contributions are free money, and missing out on them means leaving valuable savings on the table. Even if you can't afford to contribute 15% of your income right away, prioritizing at least the amount required to get the full employer match is a great starting point.

Balancing Retirement Savings With Other Financial Goals

Retirement savings should be a top priority, but it doesn't exist in isolation—you also need to prepare for unexpected expenses that could derail your financial stability. One of the main financial buffers is an emergency fund. This prevents the need to dip into retirement savings in case of job loss, medical emergencies, or unexpected expenses.

For many individuals, it can be challenging to balance retirement savings, emergency funds, and other financial goals, such as paying off debt or saving for a home. A helpful approach is to break it down into manageable percentages:

- 15% for retirement savings

- 5-10% for emergency funds (if not yet fully built)

- The remainder for necessary expenses, debt payments, and discretionary spending

A key principle to remember is that saving even small amounts consistently is more effective than waiting until you can contribute large sums. Retirement planning is a long-term effort, and steady contributions, even if they seem minor, will accumulate significantly over time.

Utilizing Tax-Advantaged Accounts

Tax-advantaged retirement accounts offer opportunities to grow savings more efficiently by reducing tax liabilities and maximizing investment gains. The two primary types of accounts to consider are:

- **Traditional 401(k) and IRA:** Contributions reduce taxable income in the year they are made, lowering tax liability. Taxes are paid upon withdrawal in retirement, ideally when you may be in a lower tax bracket.

- **Roth 401(k) and Roth IRA:** Contributions are made with after-tax dollars, but withdrawals, including investment gains, are completely tax-free in retirement.

Choosing between a traditional and Roth account depends on factors such as your current income level, expected retirement income, and tax strategy. If you anticipate being in a higher tax bracket later, a Roth IRA may be preferable, while those expecting lower taxable income in retirement might benefit more from Traditional accounts.

For those with high-deductible health plans (HDHPs), contributing to a Health Savings Account (HSA) can also be a smart financial move. HSAs offer triple tax advantages. Contributions are tax-deductible, growth is tax-free, and qualified withdrawals for medical expenses remain untaxed. These accounts can also serve as a secondary retirement savings vehicle, as unused funds roll over indefinitely and can be used for healthcare costs in retirement.

Additionally, catch-up contributions allow individuals 50 and older to contribute extra to their retirement accounts beyond standard annual limits. Taking advantage of this option can help close savings gaps and boost retirement funds in later years.

Monitoring and Adjusting Retirement Savings Plans

Planning for retirement is not a one-time event. It's an ongoing process that requires regular adjustments to stay aligned with financial goals. As life changes and economic conditions shift, staying proactive about evaluating your progress, anticipating expenses, and adapting your savings strategy ensures that you remain on track for a comfortable and secure retirement.

Evaluating Retirement Milestones

One of the most effective ways to gauge retirement readiness is by comparing your savings to established financial benchmarks. These benchmarks serve as checkpoints, helping you assess whether you are on track or need to adjust your contributions.

For example:

- **By age 30:** Aim to have savings equivalent to your annual salary.

- **By age 40:** Have at least three times your yearly salary.

- **By age 50:** Work toward accumulating five to six times your annual salary.

- **By retirement age (65+):** Target eight to ten times your salary, depending on lifestyle expectations.

Regularly reviewing where you stand compared to these benchmarks allows you to adjust your savings strategy before it's too late. If you find that you are behind schedule, consider increasing contributions, rebalancing investments for higher growth, or delaying major discretionary expenses to redirect funds into savings.

Planning for Healthcare Costs in Retirement

Healthcare is one of the biggest financial concerns for retirees, and many people underestimate how much they will need. While Medicare provides a foundation, it doesn't cover everything. Expenses like dental care, vision care, and long-term care often require additional savings or supplemental insurance.

A few key considerations:

- **Medicare premiums and out-of-pocket expenses:** Understanding the cost structure of Medicare Part B, Part D, and Medigap plans helps in estimating future healthcare costs.

- **Inflation in medical costs:** Healthcare expenses often rise faster than the general inflation rate, meaning today's estimates may not reflect future realities.

- **Long-term care planning:** Assisted living, nursing homes, and in-home care services are not covered by Medicare. Long-term care insurance or alternative savings strategies should be considered part of your plan.

By including healthcare cost projections in your retirement budget early on, you can build a financial cushion and avoid unexpected medical expenses draining your savings.

Adjusting for Inflation and Cost of Living

One of the biggest threats to retirement savings is inflation, which erodes the purchasing power of your money over time. A retirement plan that looks solid today may fall short 20 or 30 years down the road if it doesn't account for inflation.

Some strategies to combat inflation:

- Investing in assets with long-term growth potential (such as stocks or real estate) helps offset rising costs.

- Treasury Inflation-Protected Securities (TIPS) are designed to keep pace with inflation, making them a reliable option for those looking for lower-risk investments.

- Adjusting withdrawal strategies by considering a percentage-based withdrawal strategy to account for inflationary changes instead of taking a fixed dollar amount each year.

By making inflation-conscious choices, you can maintain your standard of living throughout retirement rather than watching savings diminish in value.

Managing Longevity Risk

With increasing life expectancies, outliving savings is a real concern. Retirement savings should be structured to last through 25-30 years or more. Planning for longevity requires a mix of guaranteed income sources and growth-oriented investments.

Ways to manage longevity risk:

- **Annuities:** These can provide a steady income stream for life, ensuring you don't outlive your money.

- **Diverse income streams:** Relying on multiple sources, such as Social Security, investment withdrawals, and passive income, creates stability.

- **Safe withdrawal rates:** The 4% withdrawal rule (where you withdraw 4% of your total savings annually) is a widely used strategy, but it may need adjustment depending on market conditions and personal needs.

Planning for a long retirement means making wise investment decisions and ensuring savings last as long as you need them.

Regularly Reviewing and Adjusting Your Plan

A retirement plan should never be static. Life events, economic shifts, and personal financial changes require periodic reassessments to stay aligned with your goals. Some key times to revisit your plan include:

- After significant life changes (marriage, divorce, children, relocation, etc.).

- When income levels change (promotion, job loss, new investments).

- During significant market events (recession, market crashes, economic upturns).

- At least once a year, as part of an annual financial check-in.

Adjustments might involve increasing contributions, rebalancing investments, or changing spending habits. Staying engaged with your retirement planning ensures you're never caught off guard by financial surprises.

Planning for Post-Retirement Income

Saving for retirement is only part of the equation—once you retire, managing your finances effectively becomes just as important. Your goal should be to create a sustainable withdrawal strategy that ensures your money lasts throughout your lifetime. By identifying income sources, planning smart withdrawals, and budgeting for changing expenses, you can build a stable financial future that supports your lifestyle and long-term needs.

Understanding Sources of Retirement Income

A strong retirement plan is built on multiple income streams. Most retirees rely on a combination of sources, including Social Security, retirement accounts, personal savings, and alternative income streams. Understanding the tax implications and withdrawal strategies for each can significantly impact how much you have available to spend.

Common income sources include:

- **Social Security:** Provides a guaranteed income, but varies based on when you start collecting. Delaying benefits until full retirement age—or even until age 70—can increase your monthly payments.

- **401(k) and IRA Withdrawals:** Traditional accounts are taxed as ordinary income, while Roth accounts allow for tax-free withdrawals. Managing these accounts carefully helps reduce unnecessary taxes.

- **Brokerage Accounts and Dividends:** Income from stocks, bonds, or mutual funds may be subject to lower long-term capital gains tax rates rather than ordinary income tax rates.

- **Alternative Income Sources:** Part-time work, consulting, rental properties, or passive business investments can supplement retirement savings while keeping you mentally and socially engaged.

Timing your withdrawals is key. Pulling from taxable, tax-deferred, and tax-free accounts in the right order can help minimize taxes and extend your savings.

Developing a Withdrawal Strategy

Once your income sources are identified, the next step is determining how much to withdraw each year to maintain financial stability.

The 4% Rule

A common guideline suggests withdrawing 4% of your portfolio each year and adjusting for inflation to ensure your money lasts at least 30 years. For example, if you have $1 million saved, your first-year withdrawal would be $40,000, with future withdrawals adjusted for inflation.

This rule provides a structured approach, but it may need to be adjusted based on market performance and individual spending needs.

The Total Return Approach

This method involves reinvesting dividends and interest earnings by selling a portion of investments strategically for income. Instead of relying solely on fixed withdrawals, this approach offers flexibility, allowing you to adjust spending based on market conditions while preserving your investment base.

Other considerations for structuring withdrawals include:

- Spending more in early retirement (when travel and entertainment costs may be higher) and adjusting later for reduced activity levels.

- Factoring in Required Minimum Distributions (RMDs) from tax-deferred accounts starting at age 73, to avoid penalties.

A well-planned withdrawal strategy helps maintain financial security and flexibility, ensuring that savings last while supporting your desired lifestyle.

Budgeting for Variable Expenses

Your spending habits will shift throughout retirement, making flexible budgeting essential. Some costs will decrease. Such as commuting and work-related expenses. While others, such as healthcare, may rise.

Key categories to budget for:

- **Healthcare Costs:** Medical expenses tend to increase with age, and Medicare doesn't cover everything. Consider budgeting for:

  ○ medicare premiums and out-of-pocket costs

○ prescription drug plans (Part D)

○ supplemental insurance (Medigap)

○ long-term care expenses

● **Housing Adjustments:** Many retirees downsize or relocate for lower living costs and reduced maintenance. Planning for property taxes, rent, or assisted living options is crucial.

● **Lifestyle & Leisure:** Travel and entertainment expenses may peak early in retirement but decline over time. A flexible budget ensures you can enjoy experiences without financial stress later on.

Regularly reviewing and adjusting your budget helps maintain a balance between essential expenses and discretionary spending as your retirement progresses.

Maintaining a Financial Safety Net

Unexpected expenses can disrupt even the best-laid financial plans. Having a buffer fund helps protect your retirement savings from market downturns and emergencies.

Best practices for financial security:

• Keep six to twelve months' worth of expenses in a high-yield savings account for easy access in emergencies.

• Avoid withdrawing from investment accounts during market downturns to prevent selling assets at a loss.

- Use a cash reserve strategy to cover short-term needs while allowing long-term investments to continue growing.

A well-maintained emergency fund reduces stress and financial risk, allowing you to enjoy retirement without constantly worrying about unexpected costs.

Adjusting Your Plan Over Time

Retirement is a dynamic phase of life. Your financial needs will evolve as you move through different stages. The early years may involve more active spending, while later years require adjustments for healthcare, longevity planning, and estate considerations.

Regular Financial Check-Ins

- Annual reviews ensure your withdrawal rate aligns with spending patterns.

- Market fluctuations may require adjustments in asset allocation and spending habits.

- Healthcare needs often increase, making periodic adjustments to insurance and budgeting necessary.

Long-Term Financial Planning

- Rebalancing investments keeps your portfolio aligned with your goals and risk tolerance.

- Considering annuities or longevity insurance can provide guaranteed lifetime income to protect against outliving savings.

- Estate planning ensures assets are allocated efficiently, reducing tax burdens for heirs.

By staying proactive, you can adapt to changing circumstances and maintain financial security throughout retirement.

Bringing It All Together

Planning for retirement isn't just about setting money aside. It's about creating a system that makes saving second nature while ensuring flexibility as life evolves. In this chapter, we explored how to integrate retirement savings into your budget, treating contributions like any other fixed expense to build consistency over time. Automating these savings removes the guesswork, helping young professionals and families prioritize their future selves without having to think about it every month. Retirement isn't just about reaching a savings goal. It's about creating a plan that supports your lifestyle, priorities, and peace of mind throughout the years ahead. With the right approach, you can confidently navigate your financial future, ensuring that the years you've worked so hard for are spent comfortably and worry-free.

INCLUDED: MONEY SKILLS BONUS VAULT

For additional resources and free downloads included with your book purchase, visit **https://www.pantheonspace.com/moneyskillsbonus**

These include helpful tools like:

- **Budget Template Pack** — A printable worksheet and digital tracker to plan your income, expenses, and savings

- **101-Term Budget & Money Glossary** — Key terms made simple, with beginner-friendly definitions across five core money topics

- **Quick Guide to Financial Apps & Tools** — A curated list of apps for budgeting, saving, tracking expenses, and building credit

- **Money Confidence Quiz & Habit Tracker** — Reflect on your financial habits and build stronger ones with our 30-day tracker

You can download each item directly, or view them all in one place via Google Drive. No signup is required — just helpful resources designed to boost your financial confidence.

Be notified of new releases and special promotions at
www.amazon.com/author/xyz

Keep the conversation going by joining
www.facebook.com/pantheonspace

CONCLUSION

Y ou've made it to the end of this book, and I just want to take a moment to say—look at you! You took the time to invest in yourself and your financial future, and that's something worth celebrating. Whether you started this journey feeling overwhelmed or simply curious, you're here now, equipped with the tools and knowledge to take control of your money and your life.

We all crave financial freedom, don't we? You're not alone in wanting stability and peace of mind. And guess what? By making it this far, you've already taken the first big step: paying attention to your finances and being intentional with your choices. That's huge.

Budgeting isn't just about numbers on a spreadsheet; it's about you deciding what matters most and making sure your money supports those priorities. Think of your budget as a map. Sure, there might be detours or unexpected bumps along the way, but now you have the directions to get where you want to go.

But let's be real, this isn't a one-and-done deal. Building healthy money habits takes time, patience, and (yes) some trial and error. There will be months when things click and you feel on top of the world, and others when life throws you an unexpected curveball. That's okay. The goal isn't perfection, it's progress. And every step you take toward managing your money better is a win worth acknowledging.

Discipline might sound like a tough word, but here's the truth: it's just about following through on the promises you make to yourself. Want to save more? Spend less? Pay off that loan faster? Discipline is what helps you turn those goals from "maybe someday" into "I'm doing this." And with each small victory, whether it's sticking to your grocery budget or watching your savings account grow, you'll feel that momentum build. That feeling of progress? It's addictive (in the best way).

And don't forget: this isn't just about dollars and cents, it's about creating the life you want. Perhaps that means being able to say yes to spontaneous weekend trips, supporting your loved ones, or simply going to sleep without financial worries weighing on you. Whatever your "why" is, hold onto it. Let it fuel you on the days when motivation feels hard to find.

But what about the future? That's where continuous learning comes in. Personal finance isn't static. The world changes, your goals evolve, and new opportunities (and challenges) will pop up. So, stay curious, keep asking questions, and keep learning. That's how you'll stay ahead and make choices that serve you well.

Look, I won't sugarcoat it. There will be setbacks. Days when you overspend or unexpected expenses emerge, or times when progress feels slow. Don't let those moments define you. Instead, treat them as learning experiences. Pause, reflect, adjust, and keep going. You're more resilient than you think. You've got this.

And here's something important to remember: you're not alone in this journey. So many people are trying to figure things out just like you. Talk to friends. Join communities. Share your wins (and struggles) because support and accountability make the road a whole lot easier, and honestly, more fun.

I'm genuinely proud of you for making it here. Taking charge of your finances isn't always easy, but you've proven you're up for the challenge. Every decision you make today lays the groundwork for a more secure, more empowered tomorrow. Keep going. Keep believing in yourself. Financial freedom isn't just a dream; it's something you're actively creating, one step at a time.

So as you close this book, carry this with you: you have everything you need to succeed. Stay committed, stay curious, and most importantly, stay kind to yourself along the way. Here's to a future where you call the shots, live life on your terms, and enjoy the peace of mind you deserve.

Be proud of how far you've come. I believe in you.

STUDENT BUDGET TEMPLATE

Student Budgeting Tips

- **Use a Weekly Spending Limit:** Break your variable expenses into weekly amounts to avoid overspending early in the month.

- **Textbook Alternatives:** Rent textbooks, buy used ones, or use digital versions to save significantly.

- **Maximize Campus Resources:** Take advantage of free campus resources like the library, gym, and workshops to cut costs.

- **Emergency Fund Priority:** Build a small emergency fund as a financial safety net before focusing on larger savings goals.

- **Track Expenses Consistently:** Use a simple app or spreadsheet to monitor spending daily for better control.

Income

Source	Amount (Monthly)	Notes
Part-Time Job		Income from any part-time work or campus job. Include net pay (after tax).
Allowance		Monthly financial support from family or guardians.
Scholarships/Grants		Only list the amount used for living expenses if applicable.
Student Loans (Living Expenses Portion)		If using loans for living expenses, calculate a monthly allocation.
Other Income		Freelance work, tutoring, resale of items, or other side hustles.
Total Income		

Fixed Expenses

Category	Amount (Monthly)	Notes
Tuition (Monthly Equivalent)		If tuition is paid per semester, divide it into monthly amounts for tracking purposes.
Rent/Dorm Fee		Include utilities if applicable. For on-campus housing, check what's included.
Utilities		If living off-campus, estimate electricity, water, internet, and phone costs.
Insurance		Health and renter's insurance, if applicable.
Subscriptions		Music, video streaming, study apps, and cloud services.

Transportation (Monthly Pass)		Public transport, gas, or rideshare costs. Include bike rentals if applicable.
Total Fixed Expenses		

Variable Expenses

Category	Amount (Monthly)	Notes
Groceries		Track meals and snacks purchased outside of meal plans.
Dining Out		Eating out with friends, coffee shops, and takeout. Monitor for overspending.
Course Materials/Books		Budget for books, lab fees, and other academic supplies.

Social Activities		Parties, outings, hobbies, and entertainment. Keep it reasonable to avoid budget strain.
Clothing		Budget for seasonal or essential clothing items.
Health & Wellness		Gym memberships, sports, or wellness activities. Include pharmacy expenses if needed.
Miscellaneous		Personal care items, gifts, pet costs, or one-off expenses.
Total Variable Expenses		

Savings Goals

Category	Target Amount	Current Amount	Notes
Emergency Fund			Aim to build at least $500 initially, then increase as your budget allows.
Summer Fund			Save in advance for summer expenses or unpaid internships.
Travel Fund			Budget for spring break, trips home, or study-abroad opportunities.
Future Goals			Saving for a car, post-graduation plans, or moving expenses.
Total Savings			

Summary

Category	Amount (Monthly)	Notes
Total Income		The sum of all income sources listed above. Ensure it's accurate and up to date.
Total Fixed Expenses		Fixed expenses are more predictable and should remain consistent.
Total Variable Expenses		Monitor closely— variable spending is where savings can be optimized.
Total Savings		Even small amounts saved monthly can grow significantly over time.
Net Amount (Income – Total Expenses & Savings)		A positive balance means you're managing well. If negative, adjust variable expenses or save less temporarily.

PROFESSIONAL BUDGET TEMPLATE

Professional Budgeting Tips

- **Automate Payments & Savings:** Simplify your finances by automating your bill payments and transferring a percentage of your income to savings.

- **Review Quarterly:** Check your budget every three months to account for changes in salary, lifestyle, or unexpected expenses.

- **Prioritize Debt Elimination:** Focus on high-interest debt first while contributing to long-term savings.

- **Maximize Retirement Contributions:** Take full advantage of employer-matching contributions to retirement plans like 401(k) or similar accounts.

Income

Source	Amount (Monthly)	Notes
Primary Salary		Regular paycheck after tax. Make sure to check your net income (post-tax).
Side Hustle/Freelance		Include any freelance projects, consulting gigs, or passive income (like rental or dividends).
Bonuses/Commissions		These can be irregular; consider saving a percentage for long-term goals.
Other Income		Investments, dividends, or other recurring income sources, alimony, child support, etc.
Total Income		

Fixed Expenses

Category	Amount (Monthly)	Notes
Mortgage/Rent		Include your monthly housing payment. If renting, note if utilities are included.
Utilities		Average of electricity, water, gas, internet, and phone bills.
Insurance (Health/Life)		Health, life, home, car, and disability insurance should be listed separately.
Subscriptions		Streaming services (Netflix, Spotify), gym memberships, software subscriptions, etc.
Loan Payments		Regular payments for personal loans, student loans, car loans, or credit card minimums.

Other Fixed Expenses		Childcare, tuition, or any fixed donations and charity commitments.
Total Fixed Expenses		

Variable Expenses

Category	Amount (Monthly)	Notes
Groceries		Average monthly spend. Use past receipts or credit card statements for accuracy.
Dining Out		Restaurants, coffee shops, and takeout. Monitor for potential overspending.
Transportation (Gas, Public Transit)		Include gas, public transportation, parking fees, and ride-sharing services.

Entertainment		Concerts, movies, weekend activities, hobbies, and subscriptions to events.
Clothing		Work attire, casual clothing, and accessories. Consider seasonal variations.
Health & Wellness		Gym memberships, yoga classes, vitamins, supplements, and wellness activities.
Miscellaneous		Gifts, unexpected purchases, pet expenses, or other irregular costs.
Total Variable Expenses		

Savings Goals

Category	Target Amount	Current Amount	Notes
Emergency Fund			Aim for 3-6 months of living expenses in a high-yield savings account.
Retirement Savings (401k/IRA)			Contribute enough to get your employer's match. Target 15% of your income if possible.
Vacation Fund			Save for upcoming trips to avoid credit card debt. Plan realistic timelines for funding.

Large Purchase Fund			Examples can include saving for a car, a home down payment, or a major appliance replacement.
Investment Fund			For stocks, ETFs, or mutual funds. Start small but remain consistent.
Total Savings			

Summary

Category	Amount (Monthly)	Notes
Total Income		The sum of all income sources listed above. Ensure it matches your actual inflow.

Total Fixed Expenses		This should remain stable; monitor for any annual increases.
Total Variable Expenses		Monitor this regularly to identify unnecessary spending.
Total Savings		Ensure at least 20% of your income goes toward savings and debt repayment.
Net Amount (Income – Total Expenses & Savings)		The balance should ideally be positive. Adjust variable expenses or savings contributions if necessary.

BEGINNER BUDGET TEMPLATE

Beginner Budgeting Tips

- **Track Every Expense:** In the beginning, it's crucial to track every dollar to understand spending patterns.

- **Set Realistic Savings Goals:** Start small with your emergency fund and build gradually.

- **Avoid Lifestyle Inflation:** Just because your income grows doesn't mean your expenses should increase proportionally.

- **Use Cash for Budgeting:** Consider the envelope method for variable expenses to stay disciplined.

Income

Source	Amount (Monthly)	Notes
Salary/Wages		Include net pay (after tax). For those just starting, it might be an entry-level or hourly job.
Side Hustles		Earnings from freelance work, part-time gigs, or selling items.
Support/Allowance		Financial support from family or external sources.
Total Income		

Fixed Expenses

Category	Amount (Monthly)	Notes
Rent		Housing costs. If you share rent, list your portion only.
Utilities		Electricity, water, internet, and phone services.
Insurance		Health, renters', or auto insurance.
Subscriptions		Streaming services, fitness apps, and other recurring expenses.
Transportation		Public transport, gas, or car insurance. Consider carpooling to save.
Total Fixed Expenses		

Variable Expenses

Category	Amount (Monthly)	Notes
Groceries		Essential food and household items. Stick to a grocery list.
Dining Out		Eating at restaurants or ordering takeout.
Entertainment		Movies, concerts, social outings. Budget carefully.
Shopping		Clothing, accessories, and gifts.
Personal Care		Haircuts, skincare, and wellness activities.
Total Variable Expenses		

Savings Goals

Category	Target Amount	Current Amount	Notes
Emergency Fund			Goal: 3 months of basic expenses. Start with $500 as an initial target.
Short-Term Goal			Saving for a phone upgrade, vacation, or tech gadgets.
Long-Term Goal			Future-focused savings, like education or a car.
Total Savings			

Summary

Category	Amount (Monthly)	Notes
Total Income		
Total Fixed Expenses		
Total Variable Expenses		
Total Savings		
Net Amount (Income – Total Expenses & Savings)		Make sure it's positive or adjust discretionary spending.

Intermediate Budget Template

Intermediate Budgeting Tips

- **Maximize Tax-Advantaged Accounts:** Prioritize retirement savings and health savings accounts.

- **Create Specific Sinking Funds:** Plan for predictable future expenses like car repairs or holidays.

- **Review Your Budget Quarterly:** Revisit your budget every three months to stay aligned with changing goals.

Income

Source	Amount (Monthly)	Notes
Salary/Wages		Likely a more established role or career position with a stable income.

Side Income		Freelancing, consulting, or passive income sources.
Investments/Dividends		Regular income from investments or interest on savings.
Total Income		

Fixed Expenses

Category	Amount (Monthly)	Notes
Rent/Mortgage		Include property taxes and homeowners' insurance if applicable.
Utilities		Typical utilities like water, electricity, internet, and phone.
Insurance		Health, auto, renter's/homeowner's, and life insurance.

Subscriptions/ Memberships		Professional memberships and streaming services.
Transportation		Gas, public transport, and car maintenance.
Childcare/Education		If applicable, allocate funds for childcare or education expenses.
Total Fixed Expenses		

Variable Expenses

Category	Amount (Monthly)	Notes
Groceries		Consider planning meals to avoid overspending.
Dining Out		Eating out for social or business-related purposes.
Entertainment		Include hobbies and recreational activities.

Travel		Monthly allocation for weekend trips or planned vacations.
Shopping		Clothing, tech, and household upgrades.
Health & Fitness		Gym memberships, wellness programs, and supplements.
Total Variable Expenses		

Savings and Investments

Category	Target Amount	Current Amount	Notes
Emergency Fund			Aim for 6 months of living expenses.
Retirement Savings			Contributions to 401(k), IRA, or other retirement plans.

Vacation Fund			Save for leisure without affecting other goals.
Investment Fund			Set aside money for future investments.
Total Savings			

Summary

Category	Amount (Monthly)	Notes
Total Income		Include all regular and variable income sources.
Total Fixed Expenses		Rent, utilities, insurance, subscriptions.
Total Variable Expenses		Groceries, transport, entertainment, etc.

Total Savings		Emergency fund, retirement, and short-term goals.
Net Amount (Income – Total Expenses & Savings)		Make sure it's positive or adjust discretionary spending.

ADVANCED BUDGET TEMPLATE

Advanced Budgeting Tips

- **Prioritize Wealth Preservation:** Focus on asset protection strategies.

- **Diversify Income Streams:** Look into alternative investments like crypto, art, or venture capital.

- **Work with Financial Professionals:** Regularly consult tax advisors and wealth managers.

- **Plan for Legacy:** Develop a long-term wealth transfer plan for future generations.

Income

Source	Amount (Monthly)	Notes
Salary		Likely a high-level or executive role with multiple income streams.

Business Income		Earnings from business ventures or side projects.
Investments/Dividends		Income from stocks, real estate, and other investment vehicles.
Rental Income		If applicable, list rental property earnings.
Total Income		

Fixed Expenses

Category	Amount (Monthly)	Notes
Mortgage/Rent		Include multiple properties if applicable.
Utilities		Cover all properties or business-related expenses.
Insurance		Comprehensive insurance: health, life,

		auto, liability, and property.
Professional Services		Financial advisor, tax consultant, and legal services.
Subscriptions/ Memberships		Premium services, fitness clubs, or professional organizations.
Childcare/Education		Private school tuition or extracurricular activities.
Total Fixed Expenses		

Variable Expenses

Category	Amount (Monthly)	Notes
Groceries		Consider planning meals to avoid overspending.

Dining Out		Eating out for social or business-related purposes.
Entertainment		Include hobbies and recreational activities.
Travel		Monthly allocation for weekend trips or planned vacations.
Shopping		Clothing, tech, and household upgrades.
Health & Fitness		Gym memberships, wellness programs, and supplements.
Total Variable Expenses		

Advanced Investments & Wealth Building

Category	Target Amount	Current Amount	Notes
Retirement Savings			Maximize all available tax-advantaged accounts.
Real Estate Investments			Set aside for property acquisition or upgrades.
Business Expansion Fund			Capital for scaling businesses or new ventures.
Legacy/Inheritance Fund			Plan for wealth transfer or family trusts.
Total Savings			

Summary

Category	Amount (Monthly)	Notes
Total Income		
Total Fixed Expenses		
Total Variable Expenses		
Total Savings		
Net Amount (Income – Total Expenses & Savings)		Ensure surplus funds or adjust spending/income plans.

REFERENCES

Amerant Bank Editorial Team. (2025, January 26). *Debt Management Strategies for Financial Freedom in 2025*. Amerant Bank. https://www.amerantbank.com/ofinterest/debt-management-strategies-for-financial-freedom-2025/

Anania, K. (2024, October 21). *Combining Finances As a Newly Married Couple*. Investopedia. https://www.investopedia.com/articles/personal-finance/030716/managing-money-couple.asp

An essential guide to building an emergency fund. (n.d.). Consumer Financial Protection Bureau. https://www.consumerfinance.gov/an-essential-guide-to-building-an-emergency-fund/

Bai, R. (2023). Impact of financial literacy, mental budgeting and self control on financial wellbeing: Mediating impact of investment decision making. *PLOS ONE, 18*(11), e0294466–e0294466. https://doi.org/10.1371/journal.pone.0294466

Ballinger, J. (2024, May 15). *Strategic budgeting: are you getting it right? A guide for 2024.* Cube Software. https://www.cubesoftware.com/blog/strategic-budgeting

Bartlett, B. (2024, March 2). *Essential Budgeting Tips for New Freelancers.* Medium. https://bradleebartlett.medium.com/essential-budgeting-tips-for-new-freelancers-8b93243b6ea9

Becker, S. (2023, November 7). *6 Investment Risk Management Strategies.* SoFi. https://www.sofi.com/learn/content/investment-risk-management/

Bennett, R. (2023, June 6). *5 ways to grow your savings with automatic transfers.* Bankrate. https://www.bankrate.com/banking/savings/grow-your-savings-with-automatic-transfers/

Budgeting 101. (n.d.). University of Richmond. https://financialaid.richmond.edu/financial-wellness/budgeting.html

Budgeting Strategies for a Prosperous New Year. (2023, December 19). Benchmark FCU. https://benchmarkfcu.org/budgeting-strategies/

Career Guidance Advice. (2024, October 15). *How to Successfully Budget for a Career Change.* Career Guidance Advice.

https://careerguidanceadvice.com/how-to-successfully-budget-for-a-career-change/

Cruze, R. (2024, April 16). *How to Budget by Cash Stuffing Envelopes*. Ramsey Solutions. https://www.ramseysolutions.com/budgeting/envelope-system-explained

Emergency Fund Calculator. (2020). Fifth Third Bank. https://www.53.com/content/fifth-third/en/personal-banking/planning/financial-calculators/emergency-fund-calculator.html

Evaluating Your Finances. (2024). Practical Money Skills. https://www.practicalmoneyskills.com/en/learn/budgeting/evaluating-your-finances.html

Fernando, J. (2024, June 29). *Financial literacy: What It Is, and Why It Is So important To Teach Teens*. Investopedia. https://www.investopedia.com/terms/f/financial-literacy.asp

Fidelity Viewpoints. (2024, April 15). *50/15/5: An easy trick for saving and spending*. Fidelity. https://www.fidelity.com/viewpoints/personal-finance/spending-and-saving

Financial Terms Glossary. (n.d.). Consumer Financial Protection Bureau. https://www.consumerfinance.gov/consumer-tools/educator-tools/youth-financial-education/glossary/

Find financial literacy activities. (2023, August 29). Consumer Financial Protection Bureau. https://www.consumerfinance.gov/consumer-tools/educator-tools/youth-financial-education/teach/activities/

5 Retirement Planning Strategies for Rising Healthcare Costs. (2024, October 16). Morris Financial Concepts. https://mfcplanners.com/retirement-planning-strategies-for-rising-healthcare-costs/

5 Steps to Creating an Emergency Fund. (2024, December 19). Morgan Stanley. https://www.morganstanley.com/articles/how-to-build-an-emergency-fund

5 Tips for Finding the Financial Tools that Best Fit Your Goals. (2022, January 27). PNC Insights. https://www.pnc.com/insights/personal-finance/save/5-tips-for-finding-the-financial-tools-that-best-fit-your-goals.html

Fontinelle, A. (2024, February 25). *How to Set Financial Goals for Your Future.* Investopedia. https://www.investopedia.com/articles/personal-finance/100516/setting-financial-goals/

Ganti, A. (2024, May 17). *What Is a Budget? Plus 11 Budgeting Myths Holding You Back.* Investopedia. https://www.investopedia.com/terms/b/budget.asp

Glossary of budget terms. (n.d.). Office of Financial Management. https://ofm.wa.gov/budget/glossary-budget-terms

Guardian Editorial Team. (2024). *Retirement income planning: 5 steps to success.* GuardianLife. https://www.guardianlife.com/retirement/income-planning

Harmon, R. (2025, February 24). *The 7 Best Money Saving Apps Reviewed for 2025.* TechRepublic. https://www.techrepublic.com/article/best-money-saving-apps/

How Can I Make Saving for Retirement Part of a Monthly Budget? (2024, October 22). Harvest Wealth Partners. https://www.harvestwp.com/how-can-i-make-saving-for-retirement-part-of-a-monthly-budget/

How Much Should I Keep in an Emergency Fund? (2022, February 6). Mid Penn Bank. https://midpennbank.com/what-size-emergency-fund-do-you-need/

How To Avoid — or Break — the Debt Trap Cycle. (n.d.). Office of Financial Readiness. https://finred.usalearning.gov/Money/DebtTraps

How to budget 101: 6 strategies to try. (2022, March 15). U.S. Bank. https://www.usbank.com/financialiq/manage-your-household/life-events/graduating-from-college/budgeting-strategies-to-consider.html

How to Pay Off Debt Faster. (n.d.). Wells Fargo. https://www.wellsfargo.com/goals-credit/smarter-credit/manage-your-debt/pay-off-debt-faster/

Hurtubise, D. (2024, November 16). *The 7 Best Budget Apps for 2025.* Spoken. https://www.spoken.io/blog/the-best-budget-apps

Ignite Healthwise, LLC Staff. (2024, July 31). *Reducing Financial Stress With Better Money Management Information.* Columbia University. https://www.columbiadoctors.org/health-library/article/reducing-financial-stress-better-money-management/

Karl, S. (2025, February 7). *YNAB vs. Mint.* Investopedia. https://www.investopedia.com/ynab-vs-mint-5179966

Lioudis, N. (2024, July 17). *The Importance of Diversification.* Investopedia. https://www.investopedia.com/investing/importance-diversification/

M1 Team. (2025, February 3). *Budgeting for Freelancers: Effective Strategies for Variable Income.* M1. https://m1.com/knowledge-bank/budgeting-for-freelancers-effective-strategies-for-variable-income/

McCann, A. (2023, November 6). *YNAB vs. Mint: A Better Way to Manage Money*. YNAB. https://www.ynab.com/blog/ynab-vs-mint-a-better-way-to-manage-money

McMullen, L. (2025, January 24). *The Best Budget Apps for 2025*. NerdWallet. https://www.nerdwallet.com/article/finance/best-budget-apps

McQueen, S. (2025, February 4). *The Ultimate Guide to Joint Finances: Strategies for Couples to Thrive Together*. My Wealth Solutions. https://mywealthsolutions.com.au/blog/planning/the-ultimate-guide-to-joint-finances/

Morah, C. (2023, December 16). *Evaluating your personal financial statement*. Investopedia. https://www.investopedia.com/articles/pf/08/evaluate-personal-financial-statement.asp

MsMoney . (2018). *Joint Financial Goals*. MsMoney . https://msmoney.com/life-planning/marriage-kids-college/joint-financial-goals/

Murphy, K. (2024, November 19). *The Advantages And Disadvantages Of Zero Based Budgeting (ZBB)*. PLANERGY . https://planergy.com/blog/advantages-and-disadvantages-of-zero-based-budgeting/

9cv9 HR and Career Blog. (2024, December 5). *How to Create an Emergency Fund for Your Career*. Medium. https://medium.com/@9cv9official/how-to-create-an-emergency-fund-for-your-career-ebe6d4802a10

Ram, M. (2024, April 25). *Eliminate Software Budget Overrun: #5 Debunking Common Myths*. Acquaint Softtech. https://acquaintsoft.com/blog/software-development-budget-overruns-common-myths

Ramsey Solutions. (2024, July 17). *How to Create a Family Budget*. Ramsey Solutions. https://www.ramseysolutions.com/budgeting/how-to-create-a-family-budget

Richards, M. (2025, February 17). *Retirement Cash Flow Management & Retirement Withdrawal Strategies*. SKWealth. https://skwealth.com/blog/retirement-cash-flow-management/

Royal, J. (2025, February 12). *Why do investors diversify their portfolios?* Bankrate. https://www.bankrate.com/investing/diversification-is-important-in-investing/

Saxo Group. (2025, February 28). *Diversification risks: 6 proven strategies for effective risk management*. Saxo Bank. https://www.home.saxo/learn/guides/diversification/diversification-risks-6-proven-strategies-for-effective-risk-management

Schmidt, R., & Walters, E. (2024, May 14). *2024 Milliman Retiree Health Cost Index*. Milliman. https://www.milliman.com/en/insight/retiree-health-cost-index-2024

Schwahn, L. (2023, October 11). *What Is the "Cash Stuffing" Envelope System?* NerdWallet. https://www.nerdwallet.com/article/finance/envelope-system

Schwahn, L. (2024a, February 16). *Budgeting 101: How to budget money*. NerdWallet. https://www.nerdwallet.com/article/finance/how-to-budget

Schwahn, L. (2024b, December 19). *How to Set Financial Goals*. NerdWallet. https://www.nerdwallet.com/article/finance/how-to-set-financial-goals

seo@southeastlegalmarketing.com. (2024, November 25). *How to Avoid Debt Traps: Tips for Staying Financially Secure*. Padgett & Robertson. https://www.hermandpadgett.com/how-to-avoid-debt-traps-tips-for-staying-financially-secure/

Short, medium, and long term goals. (2025, February 28). Khan Academy. https://www.khanacademy.org/college-careers-more/financial-literacy/xa6995ea67a8e9fdd:financial-goals/xa6995ea67a8e9fdd:short-medium-and-long-term-goals/a/short-medium-and-long-term-goals

Solutions for paying down debt: Avalanche, snowball or HELOC?. (2020, May 1). Citizens. https://www.citizensbank.com/learning/what-is-the-debt-snowball-pay-down-method.aspx

Successful Budgeting and Financial Planning for the New Year. (2025, March 3). DFPI. https://dfpi.ca.gov/news/insights/successful-budgeting-and-financial-planning-for-the-new-year/

Tabora, F. (2024, April 30). *How to make a budget in Excel*. Microsoft 365. https://create.microsoft.com/en-us/learn/articles/how-to-make-excel-budget

Team Appreciate. (2023, December 19). *Understanding different types of investments: Stocks, bonds, mutual funds, ETFs*. Appreciate. https://appreciatewealth.com/blog/understanding-different-types-of-investments-stocks-bonds-mutual-funds-etfs

Team Paidly. (2024, July 11). *The 50-30-20 Rule: How to Budget Your Way Out of Student Loan Debt*. Paidly. https://meetpaidly.com/blog/50-30-20-rule-budget-out-of-student-loan-debt

Tepper, T. (2024, November 20). *Best Budgeting Apps Of March 2025*. Forbes Advisor. https://www.forbes.com/advisor/banking/best-budgeting-apps/

13 Financial Literacy Games For Children And Adults
    (Gamification Resources). (2021, April 30). Fitzsimons
    Credit Union.
    https://www.fitzsimonscu.com/blog/financial-literacy-
    games-for-children-and-adults/

Vecchio, L. D. (2025, February 11). *Strategic Budgeting: What Is It,
    Process, and Best Practices.* Planergy Software.
    https://planergy.com/blog/strategic-budgeting/

Vives, O. (2024, October 3). *What is the best way to benchmark
    progress in retirement?* Sensible Money.
    https://www.sensiblemoney.com/learn/what-is-the-best-
    way-to-benchmark-progress-in-retirement/

Warshaw, J. (2024, April 23). *What Debt Do You Pay Off First?*
    Ramsey Solutions.
    https://www.ramseysolutions.com/debt/what-debt-do-i-
    pay-off-first

*What Are Budgeting Apps and How Do They Work? Understanding
    Budgeting Apps.* (2024, May 15). Equifax.
    https://www.equifax.com/personal/education/personal-
    finance/articles/-/learn/budgeting-apps/

What does it mean to plan your retirement? (2018). Merrill.
    https://www.ml.com/planning-for-retirement.html

*What Is Investing? A Complete Guide to Types of Investments and
    Strategies.* (2024, December 4). Royalty Exchange.

https://www.royaltyexchange.com/blog/what-is-investing-a-complete-guide-to-types-of-investments-and-strategies

Xie, A. (2024, December 10). *Zero-Based Budgeting Explained: Benefits, Examples, and Best Practices.* Go Limelight. https://www.golimelight.com/blog/zero-based-budgeting

www.ingramcontent.com/pod-product-compliance
Lightning Source LLC
Chambersburg PA
CBHW030506210326
41597CB00013B/815